THE ORGANISATION
OF THOUGHT,

EDUCATIONAL AND SCIENTIFIC

BY

A. N. WHITEHEAD, Sc.D., F.R.S.

FELLOW OF TRINITY COLLEGE, CAMBRIDGE, AND PROFESSOR OF
APPLIED MATHEMATICS AT THE IMPERIAL COLLEGE OF
SCIENCE AND TECHNOLOGY

GREENWOOD PRESS, PUBLISHERS
WESTPORT, CONNECTICUT

Library of Congress Cataloging in Publication Data

Whitehead, Alfred North, 1861-1947.
  The organisation of thought.

    Reprint of the 1917 ed. published by Williams and
Norgate, London.
    CONTENTS: The aims of education--a plea for reform.
--Technical education and its relation to science and
literature. [etc.]
    1. Education--Collected works. I. Title.
LB41.W64   370'.8   76-106727
ISBN 0-8371-3448-X

Originally published in 1917 by Williams and Norgate, London

Reprinted by Greenwood Press,
a division of Williamhouse-Regency Inc.

First Greenwood Reprinting 1974
Second Greenwood Reprinting 1975

Library of Congress Catalog Card Number 76-106727

ISBN 0-8371-3448-X

Printed in the United States of America

PREFACE

THE discourses included in this volume have been delivered as addresses on various occasions which are duly noted; the only exception is *The Anatomy of Some Scientific Ideas*, which is now published for the first time. These discourses fall into two sections, the first five chapters deal with education, and the remaining three embody discussions on certain points arising in the philosophy of science. But a common line of reflection extends through the whole, and the two sections influence each other.

I have left in each chapter the reference to the particular occasion of its first production, and I have not sought for a verbal consistency covering perplexity. But the various parts of the book were in fact composed with express reference to each other, so as to form one whole.

I have to thank the Syndics of the Cambridge University Press for permission to republish the contents of Chapter V.

Imperial College of Science and Technology,
April 1917

TABLE OF CONTENTS

ORGANISATION OF THOUGHT

CHAPTER I

THE AIMS OF EDUCATION—A PLEA FOR REFORM

(Presidential Address to the Mathematical Association, January, 1916)

WHEN I had the honour of being made President of the Mathematical Association, I did not foresee the unusual responsibility which it entailed. It was my intention to take as the theme of a presidential address the consideration of some aspect of those special subjects to which my own researches have principally been directed. Events have forced me to abandon that intention. It is useless to discuss abstract questions in the midst of dominant practical preoccupation. We cannot disregard the present crisis in European civilisation. It affects every function of life. In the harder struggle for existence which lies before the nation, all departments of national effort will be reviewed for judgment. The mere necessity for economy in resources will provoke this reformation.

We are concerned with education. This

B

Association, so rich in its membership of educationalists, with the conception of reform as the very reason of its being, is among those bodies which must take the lead in guiding that educational reconstruction which by a sociological law follows every social revolution. ⁓We do not want impracticable ideals, only to be realised beyond the clouds in

"Some wild, weird clime,
Out of Space, and out of Time."

We require to know what is possible now in England, a nation conscious of its high achievements, and of great failures, shaken to its foundations, distrustful of the old ways, and dreading fantastic novelties.

I will take my courage in both hands, and put before you an outline of educational principles. What I am going to say is of course entirely without your authority, and does not pledge or prejudge any action of the Association. We are primarily concerned only with the intellectual side of education, and, as mathematicians, are naturally concerned to illustrate details more particularly by reference to mathematics. Thus much to explain deliberate omissions in what follows.

Consider now the general and special education of two types of boys, namely those in secondary schools who in after life must form the professional and directing classes in commerce, industry, and public administration, and again those in junior technical schools and later in advanced continuation classes, who are going to form the class of skilled artisans and foremen of workshops. These two sets compose the educated strength of the nation. We must form no ideals which include less than these entire classes within their scope. What I shall say, will in phraseology apply more directly to the secondary schools, but with unessential changes it will apply equally to the other group.

What is the first commandment to be obeyed in any educational scheme? It is this : Do not teach too many subjects. The second command is this : What you teach, teach thoroughly. The devil in the scholastic world has assumed the form of a general education consisting of scraps of a large number of disconnected subjects; and, with the artfulness of the serpent, he has entrenched himself behind the matriculation examination of the University of London, with a wire entanglement formed by the Oxford and Cambridge schools' examination.

Culture is activity of thought, and receptiveness to beauty, and humane feeling. Scraps of information have nothing to do with it. A merely well-informed man is the most useless bore on God's earth. What we should aim at producing is men who possess both culture and expert

knowledge in some special direction. Their expert knowledge will give them the ground to
start from, and their culture will lead them as
deep as philosophy and as high as art. We have
to remember that the valuable intellectual
development is self-development, and that it
mostly takes place between the ages of sixteen
and thirty. As to training, the most important
part is given by mothers before the age of twelve.
A saying due to Archbishop Temple illustrates
my meaning. Surprise was expressed at the
success in after-life of a man, who as a boy at
Rugby had been somewhat undistinguished. He
answered, " It is not what they are at eighteen,
it is what they become afterwards that matters."

In training a child to activity of thought,
above all things we must beware of what I will
call "inert ideas "—that is to say, ideas that
are merely received into the mind without
being utilised, or tested, or thrown into fresh
combinations.

In the history of education, the most striking
phenomenon is that schools of learning, which
at one epoch are alive with a ferment of genius,
in a succeeding generation exhibit merely
pedantry and routine. The reason is, that they
are overladen with inert ideas. Education with
inert ideas is not only useless : it is, above all
things, harmful—*Corruptio optimi, pessima*. Except at rare intervals of intellectual ferment,

education in the past has been radically infected
with inert ideas. That is the reason why uneducated clever women, who have seen much
of the world, are in middle life so much the most
cultured part of the community. They have
been saved from this horrible burden of inert
ideas. Every intellectual revolution which has
ever stirred humanity into greatness has been a
passionate protest against inert ideas. Then,
alas, with pathetic ignorance of human psychology, it has proceeded by some educational
scheme to bind humanity afresh with inert ideas
of its own fashioning.

Let us now ask how in our system of education
we are to guard against this· mental dry rot.
We recur to our two educational commandments,
" Do not teach too many subjects," and again,
" What you teach, teach thoroughly."

The result of teaching small parts of a large
number of subjects is the passive reception of
disconnected ideas, not illumined with any spark
of vitality. Let the main ideas which are introduced into a child's education be few and important, and let them be thrown into every
combination possible. The child should make
them his own, and should understand their
application here and now in the circumstances
of his actual life. From the very beginning
of his education, the child should experience the
joy of discovery. The discovery which he has

to make, is that general ideas give an understanding of that stream of events which pours through his life, which is his life.   By understanding I mean more than a mere logical analysis, though that is included.   I mean " understanding " in the sense in which it is used in the French proverb, " To understand all, is to forgive all."   Pedants sneer at an education which is useful.   But if education is not useful, what is it ? Is it a talent, to be hidden away in a napkin ? Of course, education should be useful, whatever your aim in life.   It was useful to Saint Augustine and it was useful to Napoleon.   It is useful, because understanding is useful.

I pass lightly over that understanding which should be given by the literary side of education. It is not peculiarly the function of this Association to consider it.   Nor do I wish to be supposed to pronounce on the relative merits of a classical or a modern curriculum.   I would only remark that the understanding which we want is an understanding of an insistent present. The only use of a knowledge of the past is to equip us for the present.   No more deadly harm can be done to young minds than by depreciation of the present.   The present contains all that there is. It is holy ground; for it is the past, and it is the future. At the same time it must be observed that an age is no less past if it existed two hundred years ago than if it existed two thousand years ago. Do not be deceived by the pedantry of dates. The ages of Shakespeare and of Molière are no less past than are the ages of Sophocles and of Virgil. The communion of saints is a great and inspiring assemblage, but it has only one possible hall of meeting, and that is, the present; and the mere lapse of time through which any particular group of saints must travel to reach that meeting-place, makes very little difference.

Passing now to the scientific and logical side of education, we remember that here also ideas which are not utilised are positively harmful. By utilising an idea, I mean relating it to that stream, compounded of sense perceptions, feelings, hopes, desires, and of mental activities relating thought to thought, which forms our life. I can imagine a set of beings which might fortify their souls by passively reviewing disconnected ideas. Humanity is not built that way—except perhaps some editors of newspapers.

In scientific training, the first thing to do with an idea is to prove it. But allow me for one moment to extend the meaning of " prove "; I mean—to prove its worth. Now an idea is not worth much unless the propositions in which it is embodied are true. Accordingly an essential part of the proof of an idea is the proof, either by experiment or by logic, of the truth of the propositions. But it is not essential that this proof of the truth should constitute the first introduction to the idea. After all, its assertion by the authority of respectable teachers is sufficient evidence to begin with. In our first contact with a set of propositions, we commence by appreciating their importance. That is what we all do in after-life. We do not attempt, in the strict sense, to prove or to disprove anything, unless its importance makes it worthy of that honour. These two processes of proof, in the narrow sense, and of appreciation do not require a rigid separation in time. Both can be proceeded with nearly concurrently. But in so far as either process must have the priority, it should be that of appreciation by use.

Furthermore, we should not endeavour to use propositions in isolation. Emphatically I do not mean, a neat little set of experiments to illustrate Proposition I and then the proof of Proposition I, a neat little set of experiments to illustrate Proposition II and then the proof of Proposition II, and so on to the end of the book. Nothing could be more boring. Interrelated truths are utilised *en bloc*, and the various propositions are employed in any order, and with any reiteration. Choose some important applications of your theoretical subject; and study them concurrently with the systematic theoretical exposition. Keep the theoretical exposition short and simple, but let it be strict and rigid so far as it goes. It should not be too long for it easily to be known with thoroughness and accuracy. The consequences of a plethora of half-digested theoretical knowledge are deplorable. Also the theory should not be muddled up with the practice. The child should have no doubt when it is proving and when it is utilising. My point is that what is proved should be utilised, and that what is utilised should—so far as is practicable—be proved. I am far from asserting that proof and utilisation are the same thing.

At this point of my discourse, I can most directly carry forward my argument in the outward form of a digression. We are only just realising that the art and science of education require a genius and a study of their own; and that this genius and this science are more than a bare knowledge of some branch of science or of literature. This truth was partially perceived in the past generation; and headmasters, somewhat crudely, were apt to supersede learning in their colleagues by requiring left-hand bowling and a taste for football. But culture is more than cricket, and more than football, and more than extent of knowledge.

Education is the acquisition of the art of the utilisation of knowledge. This is an art very difficult to impart. Whenever a text-book is written of real educational worth, you may be quite certain that some reviewer will say that it

will be difficult to teach from it. Of course
it will be difficult to teach from it. If it were
easy, the book ought to be burned; for it cannot
be educational. In education, as elsewhere,
the broad primrose path leads to a nasty place.
This evil path is represented by a book or a set
of lectures which will practically enable the student to learn by heart all the questions likely
to be asked at the next external examination.
And I may say in passing that no educational
system is possible unless every question directly
asked of a pupil at any examination is either
framed or modified by the actual teacher of that
pupil in that subject. The external assessor
may report on the curriculum or on the perform-
ance of the pupils, but never should be allowed
to ask the pupil a question which has not been
strictly supervised by the actual teacher, or at
least inspired by a long conference with him.
There are a few exceptions to this rule, but they
are exceptions, and could easily be allowed for
under the general rule.

   We now return to my previous point, that
theoretical ideas should always find important
applications within the pupil's curriculum. This
is not an easy doctrine to apply, but a very hard
one. It contains within itself the problem of
keeping knowledge alive, of preventing it from
becoming inert, which is the central problem of
all education.

The best procedure will depend on several factors, none of which can be neglected, namely, the genius of the teacher, the intellectual type of the pupils, their prospects in life, the opportunities offered by the immediate surroundings of the school, and allied factors of this sort. It is for this reason that the uniform external examination is so deadly. We do not denounce it because we are cranks, and like denouncing established things. We are not so childish. Also, of course, such examinations have their use in testing slackness. Our reason of dislike is very definite and very practical. It kills the best part of culture. When you analyse in the light of experience the central task of education, you find that its successful accomplishment depends on a delicate adjustment of many variable factors. The reason is that we are dealing with human minds, and not with dead matter. The evocation of curiosity, of judgment, of the power of mastering a complicated tangle of circumstances, the use of theory in giving foresight in special cases—all these powers are not to be imparted by a set rule embodied in one schedule of examination subjects.

I appeal to you, as practical teachers. With good discipline, it is always possible to pump into the minds of a class a certain quantity of inert knowledge. You take a text-book and make them learn it. So far, so good. The child then knows how to solve a quadratic equation. But what is the point of teaching a child to solve a quadratic equation? There is a traditional answer to this question. It runs thus: The mind is an instrument, you first sharpen it, and then use it; the acquisition of the power of solving a quadratic equation is part of the process of sharpening the mind. Now there is just enough truth in this answer to have made it live through the ages. But for all its half-truth, it embodies a radical error which bids fair to stifle the genius of the modern world. I do not know who was first responsible for this analogy of the mind to a dead instrument. For aught I know, it may have been one of the seven wise men of Greece, or a committee of the whole lot of them. Whoever was the originator, there can be no doubt of the authority which it has acquired by the continuous approval which it has received from eminent persons. But whatever its weight of authority, whatever the high approval which it can quote, I have no hesitation in denouncing it as one of the most fatal, erroneous, and dangerous conceptions ever introduced into the theory of education. The mind is never passive; it is a perpetual activity, delicate, receptive, responsive to stimulus. You cannot postpone its life until you have sharpened it. Whatever interest attaches to your subject-matter, must be evoked here and now; whatever powers you are strengthening in the pupil, must be exercised here and now; whatever possibilities of mental life your teaching should impart, must be exhibited here and now. That is the golden rule of education, and a very difficult rule to follow.

The difficulty is just this : the apprehension of general ideas, intellectual habits of mind, and pleasurable interest in mental achievement can be evoked by no form of words, however accurately adjusted. All practical teachers know that education is a patient process of the mastery of details, minute by minute, hour by hour, day by day. There is no royal road to learning through an airy path of brilliant generalisations. There is a proverb about the difficulty of seeing the wood because of the trees. That difficulty is exactly the point which I am enforcing. The problem of education is to make the pupil see the wood by means of the trees.

The solution which I am urging, is to eradicate the fatal disconnection of subjects which kills the vitality of our modern curriculum. There is only one subject-matter for education, and that is Life in all its manifestations. Instead of this single unity, we offer children—Algebra, from which nothing follows; Geometry, from which nothing follows; Science, from which nothing follows; History, from which nothing follows; a Couple of Languages, never mastered; and lastly, most dreary of all, Literature, represented by plays of Shakespeare, with philological notes and short analyses of plot and character to be in substance committed to memory. Can such a list be said to represent Life, as it is known in the midst of the living of it? The best that can be said of it is, that it is a rapid table of contents which a deity might run over in his mind while he was thinking of creating a world, and had not yet determined how to put it together.

Let us now return to quadratic equations. We still have on hand the unanswered question. Why should children be taught their solution? Unless quadratic equations fit into a connected curriculum, of course there is no reason to teach anything about them. Furthermore, extensive as should be the place of mathematics in a complete culture, I am a little doubtful whether for many types of boys algebraic solutions of quadratic equations do not lie on the specialist side of mathematics. I may here remind you that as yet I have not said anything of the psychology or the content of the specialism, which is so necessary a part of an ideal education. But all that is an evasion of our real question, and I merely state it in order to avoid being misunderstood in my answer.

Quadratic equations are part of algebra, and algebra is the intellectual instrument which has been created for rendering clear the quantitative aspects of the world. There is no getting out of it. Through and through the world is infected with quantity. To talk sense, is to talk in quantities. It is no use saying that the nation is large,—How large? It is no use saying that radium is scarce,—How scarce? You cannot evade quantity. You may fly to poetry and to music, and quantity and number will face you in your rhythms and your octaves. Elegant intellects which despise the theory of quantity, are but half developed. They are more to be pitied than blamed. The scraps of gibberish, which in their school-days were taught to them in the name of algebra, deserve some contempt.

This question of the degeneration of algebra into gibberish, both in word and in fact, affords a pathetic instance of the uselessness of reforming educational schedules without a clear conception of the attributes which you wish to evoke in the living minds of the children. A few years ago there was an outcry that school algebra was in need of reform, but there was a general agreement that graphs would put everything right. So all sorts of things were extruded, and graphs were introduced. So far as I can see, with no sort of idea behind them, but just graphs. Now every examination paper has one or two questions on graphs. Personally, I am an enthusiastic adherent of graphs. But I wonder whether as yet we have gained very much. You cannot put life into any schedule of general education unless you succeed in exhibiting its relation to some essential characteristic of all intelligent or emotional perception. It is a hard saying, but it is true; and I do not see how to make it any easier. In making these little formal alterations you are beaten by the very nature of things. You are pitted against too skilful an adversary, who will see to it that the pea is always under the other thimble.

Reformation must begin at the other end. First, you must make up your mind as to those quantitative aspects of the world which are simple enough to be introduced into general education; then a schedule of algebra should be framed which will about find its exemplification in these applications. We need not fear for our pet graphs, they will be there in plenty when we once begin to treat algebra as a serious means of studying the world. Some of the simplest applications will be found in the quantities which occur in the simplest study of society. The curves of history are more vivid and more informing than the dry catalogues of names and dates which comprise the greater part of that arid school study. What purpose is effected by a catalogue of undistinguished kings and queens? Tom, Dick, or Harry, they are all dead. General resurrections are failures, and are better postponed. The quantitative flux of the forces of modern society are capable of very simple exhibition. Meanwhile, the idea of the variable, of the function, of rate of change, of equations and their solution, of elimination, are being studied as an abstract science for their own sake. Not, of course, in the pompous phrases with which I am alluding to them here, but with that iteration of simple special cases proper to teaching.

If this course be followed, the route from Chaucer to the Black Death, from the Black Death to modern Labour troubles, will connect the tales of the mediæval pilgrims with the abstract science of algebra, both yielding diverse aspects of that single theme, Life. I know what most of you are thinking at this point. It is that the exact course which I have sketched out is not the particular one which you would have chosen, or even see how to work. I quite agree. I am not claiming that I could do it myself. But your objection is the precise reason why a common external examination system is fatal to education. The process of exhibiting the applications of knowledge must, for its success, essentially depend on the character of the pupils and the genius of the teacher. Of course I have left out the easiest applications with which most of us are more at home. I mean the quantitative sides of sciences, such as mechanics and physics. My meaning can be illustrated by looking

c

more closely into a special case of this type of application. In my rough catalogue of the sort of subjects which should form the schedule for algebra, I mentioned Elimination. It was not put there by accident, for it covers a very important body of thought.

In the first place, there is the abstract process of algebraic elimination for suitable simple cases. The pupil acquires a firm grasp of this by the process, inevitable in education, of working an adequate number of examples. Again, there are the graphical solutions of the same problem. Then we consider the significance in the external world. We consider the velocity, time, space, acceleration diagrams. We take uniform acceleration; we eliminate "t" between

$$v = u + ft, \text{ and } s = ut + \tfrac{1}{2}ft^2,$$

and eliminate "s" between

$$v^2 = u^2 + 2fs, \text{ and } s = ut + \tfrac{1}{2}ft^2.$$

Then we remember that constant acceleration is a very special case, and we consider graphical solutions or empirically given variations of v or of f. In preference, we use those empirical formulæ which occur in the pupil's experimental work. We compare the strong and weak points of the algebraic and graphical solutions.

Again, in the same connection we plot the

statistics of social phenomena against the time. We then eliminate the time between suitable pairs. We can speculate how far we have exhibited a real casual connection, or how far a mere temporal coincidence. We notice that we might have plotted against the time one set of statistics for one country and another set for another country, and thus, with suitable choice of subjects, have obtained graphs which certainly exhibited mere coincidence. Also other graphs exhibit obvious casual connections. We wonder how to discriminate. And so are drawn on as far as we will.

But in considering this description, I must beg you to remember what I have been insisting on above. In the first place, one train of thought will not suit all groups of children. For example, I should expect that artisan children will want something more concrete and, in a sense, swifter than I have set down here. Perhaps I am wrong, but that is what I should guess. In the second place, I am not contemplating one beautiful lecture stimulating, once and for all, an admiring class. That is not the way in which education proceeds. No; all the time the pupils are hard at work solving examples, drawing graphs, and making experiments, until they have a thorough hold on the whole subject. I am describing the interspersed explanations, the directions which should be given to their thoughts. The pupils have got to be made to feel that they are studying something, and are not merely executing intellectual minuets.

In this connection the excellence of some of the most recent text-books on elementary algebra emanating from members of this Association, should create an epoch in the teaching of the subject.

Finally, if you are teaching pupils for some general examination, the problem of sound teaching is greatly complicated. Have you ever noticed the zig-zag moulding round a Norman arch ? The ancient work is beautiful, the modern work is hideous. The reason is, that the modern work is done to exact measure, the ancient work is varied according to the idiosyncrasy of the workman. Here it is crowded, and there it is expanded. Now the essence of getting pupils through examinations is to give equal weight to all parts of the schedule. But mankind is naturally specialist. One man sees a whole subject, where another can find only a few detached examples. I know that it seems contradictory to allow for specialism in a curriculum especially designed for a broad culture. Without contradictions the world would be simpler, and perhaps duller. But I am certain that in education wherever you exclude specialism you destroy life.

We now come to the other great branch of a

general mathematical education, namely Geometry. The same principles apply. The theoretical part should be clear-cut, rigid, short, and important. Every proposition not absolutely necessary to exhibit the main connection of ideas should be cut out, but the great fundamental ideas should be all there. No omission of concepts, such as those of Similarity and Proportion. We must remember that, owing to the aid rendered by the visual presence of a figure, Geometry is a field of unequalled excellence for the exercise of the deductive faculties of reasoning. Then, of course, there follows Geometrical Drawing, with its training for the hand and eye.

But, like Algebra, Geometry and Geometrical Drawing must be extended beyond the mere circle of geometrical ideas. In an industrial neighbourhood, machinery and workshop practice form the appropriate extension. For example, in the London Polytechnics this has been achieved with conspicuous success. For many secondary schools I suggest that surveying and maps are the natural applications. In particular, plane-table surveying should lead pupils to a vivid apprehension of the immediate application of geometric truths. Simple drawing apparatus, a surveyor's chain, and a surveyor's compass, should enable the pupils to rise from the survey and mensuration of a field to the construction of

the map of a small district.   The best education ✓
is to be found in gaining the utmost information from the simplest apparatus.   The provision
of elaborate instruments is greatly to be depre-
cated.   To have constructed the map of a small
district, to have considered its roads, its con-
tours, its geology, its climate, its relation to other
districts, the effects on the status of its inhabi-
tants, will teach more history and geography
than any knowledge of Perkin Warbeck or of
Behren's Straits.   I mean not a nebulous lecture
on the subject, but a serious investigation in
which the real facts are definitely ascertained
by the aid of accurate theoretical knowledge.
A typical mathematical problem should be :
Survey such and such a field, draw a plan of it
to such and such a scale, and find the area.   It
would be quite a good procedure to impart the
necessary geometrical propositions without their
proofs.   Then, concurrently in the same term,
the proofs of the propositions would be learnt
while the survey was being made.

Fortunately, the specialist side of education
presents an easier problem than does the provision of a general culture.   For this there are many
reasons.   One is that many of the principles of
procedure to be observed are the same in both
cases, and it is unnecessary to recapitulate.
Another reason is that specialist training takes
place—or should take place—at a more advanced

stage of the pupil's course, and thus there is easier material to work upon. But undoubtedly the chief reason is that the specialist study is normally a study of peculiar interest to the student. He is studying it because, for some reason, he wants to know it. This makes all the difference. The general culture is designed to foster an activity of mind; the specialist course utilises this activity. But it does not do to lay too much stress on these neat antitheses. As we have already seen, in the general course foci of special interest will arise; and similarly in the special study, the external connections of the subject drag thought outwards.

Again, there is not one course of study which merely gives general culture, and another which gives special knowledge. The subjects pursued for the sake of a general education are special subjects specially studied; and, on the other hand, one of the ways of encouraging general mental activity is to foster a special devotion You may not divide the seamless coat of learning What education has to impart is an intimate sense for the power of ideas, for the beauty of ideas, and for the structure of ideas, together with a particular body of knowledge which has peculiar reference to the life of the being possessing it.

The appreciation of the structure of ideas is that side of a cultured mind which can only grow under the influence of a special study. I mean that eye for the whole chess-board, for the bearing of one set of ideas on another. Nothing but a special study can give any appreciation for the exact formulation of general ideas, for their relations when formulated, for their service in the comprehension of life. A mind so disciplined should be both more abstract and more concrete. It has been trained in the comprehension of abstract thought and in the analysis of facts.

Finally, there should grow the most austere of all mental qualities; I mean the sense for style. It is an æsthetic sense, based on admiration for the direct attainment of a foreseen end, simply and without waste. Style in art, style in literature, style in science, style in logic, style in practical execution have fundamentally the same æsthetic qualities, namely, attainment and restraint. The love of a subject in itself and for itself, where it is not the sleepy pleasure of pacing a mental quarter-deck, is the love of style as manifested in that study.

Here we are brought back to the position from which we started, the utility of education. Style, in its finest sense, is the last acquirement of the educated mind; it is also the most useful. It pervades the whole being. The administrator with a sense for style, hates waste; the engineer with a sense for style, economises his material;

the artisan with a sense for style, prefers good work. Style is the ultimate morality of mind.

But above style, and above knowledge, there is something, a vague shape like fate above the Greek gods. That something is Power. Style is the fashioning of power, the restraining of power. But, after all, the power of attainment of the desired end is fundamental. The first thing is to get there. Do not bother about your style, but solve your problem, justify the ways of God to man, administer your province, or do whatever else is set before you.

Where, then, does style help? In this, with style the end is attained without side issues, without raising undesirable inflammations. With style you attain your end and nothing but your end. With style the effect of your activity is calculable, and foresight is the last gift of gods to men. With style your power is increased, for your mind is not distracted with irrelevancies and you are more likely to attain your object. Now style is the exclusive privilege of the expert. Whoever heard of the style of an amateur painter, of the style of an amateur poet? Style is always the product of specialist study, the peculiar contribution of specialism to culture.

English education in its present phase suffers from a lack of definite aim, and from an external machinery which kills its vitality. Hitherto in this address I have been considering the

which should govern education. In this res
England halts between two opinions. It i.
not decided whether to produce amateurs o
experts. The profound change in the world
which the nineteenth century has produced is
that the growth of knowledge has given foresight.
The amateur is essentially a man with appreciation and with immense versatility in mastering
a given routine. But he lacks the foresight
which comes from special knowledge. The object of this address is to suggest how to produce
the expert without loss of the essential virtues
of the amateur. The machinery of our secondary
education is rigid where it should be yielding,
and lax where it should be rigid. Every school
is bound on pain of extinction to train its boys
for a small set of definite examinations. No
headmaster has a free hand to develop his
general education or his specialist studies in
accordance with the opportunities of his school,
which are created by its staff, its environment,
its class of boys, and its endowments. I suggest
that no system of external tests which aims
primarily at examining individual scholars can
result in anything but educational waste.

Primarily it is the schools and not the scholars
which should be inspected. Each school should
grant its own leaving certificates, based on its
own curriculum. The standards of these schools
should be sampled and corrected. But the first

requisite for educational reform is the school as a unit, with its approved curriculum based on its own needs, and evolved by its own staff. If we fail to secure that, we simply fall from one formalism into another, from one dung-hill of inert ideas into another.

In stating that the school is the true educational unit in any national system for the safeguarding of efficiency, I have conceived the alternative system as being the external examination of the individual scholar. But every Scylla is faced by its Charybdis—or, in more homely language, there is a ditch on both sides of the road. It will be equally fatal to education if we fall into the hands of a supervising department which is under the impression that it can divide all schools into two or three rigid categories, each type being forced to adopt a rigid curriculum. When I say that the school is the educational unit, I mean exactly what I say, no larger unit, no smaller unit. Each school must have the claim to be considered in relation to its special circumstances. The classifying of schools for some purposes is necessary. But no absolutely rigid curriculum, not modified by its own staff, should be permissible. Exactly the same principles apply, with the proper modifications, to universities and to technical colleges.

When one considers in its length and in its breadth the importance of this question of the education of a nation's young, the broken lives, the defeated hopes, the national failures, which result from the frivolous inertia with which it is treated, it is difficult to restrain within oneself a savage rage. In the conditions of modern life the rule is absolute, the race which does not value trained intelligence is doomed. Not all your heroism, not all your social charm, not all your wit, not all your victories on land or at sea, can move back the finger of fate. To-day we maintain ourselves. To-morrow science will have moved forward yet one more step, and there will be no appeal from the judgment which will then be pronounced on the uneducated.

We can be content with no less than the old summary of educational ideal which has been current at any time from the dawn of our civilisation. The essence of education is that it be religious.

Pray, what is religious education?

A religious education is an education which inculcates duty and reverence. Duty arises from our potential control over the course of events. Where attainable knowledge could have changed the issue, ignorance has the guilt of vice. And the foundation of reverence is this perception, that the present holds within itself the complete sum of existence, backwards and forwards, that whole amplitude of time, which is eternity.

CHAPTER II

*(Presidential Address to the Mathematical
Association, January, 1917)*

THE subject of this address is Technical Education. I wish to examine its essential nature and also its relation to a liberal education. Such an inquiry may help us to realise the conditions for the successful working of a national system of technical training. It is also a very burning question among mathematical teachers; for mathematics is included in most technological courses.

Now it is unpractical to plunge into such a discussion without framing in our own minds the best ideal towards which we desire to work, however modestly we may frame our hopes as to the result which in the near future is likely to be achieved.

People are shy of ideals; and accordingly we find a formulation of the ideal state of mankind placed by a modern dramatist[1] in the mouth of a

---

[1] *Cf.* BERNARD SHAW: *John Bull's Other Island.*

mad priest : " In my dreams it is a country where the State is the Church and the Church the people: three in one and one in three.   It is a common-wealth in which work is play and play is life : three in one and one in three.   It is a temple in which the priest is the worshipper and the wor-shipper the worshipped : three in one and one in three.   It is a godhead in which all life is human and all humanity divine : three in one and one in three.   It is, in short, the dream of a madman."

Now the part of this speech to which I would direct attention is embodied in the phrase, " It is a commonwealth in which work is play and play is life."   This is the ideal of technical educa-tion.   It sounds very mystical when we confront it with the actual facts, the toiling millions, tired, discontented, mentally indifferent, and then the employers—— I am not undertaking a social analysis, but I shall carry you with me when I admit that the present facts of society are a long way off this ideal.   Furthermore, we are agreed that an employer who conducted his workshop on the principle that " work should be play " would be ruined in a week.

The curse that has been laid on humanity, in fable and in fact, is, that by the sweat of its brow shall it live.   But reason and moral intui-tion have seen in this curse the foundation for advance.   The early Benedictine monks rejoiced in their labours because they conceived themselves as thereby made fellow-workers with Christ.

Stripped of its theological trappings, the essential idea remains, that work should be transfused with intellectual and moral vision and thereby turned into a joy, triumphing over its weariness and its pain. Each of us will re-state this abstract formulation in a more concrete shape in accordance with his private outlook. State it how you like, so long as you do not lose the main point in your details. However you phrase it, it remains the sole real hope of toiling humanity; and it is in the hands of technical teachers, and of those who control their spheres of activity, so to mould the nation that daily it may pass to its labours in the spirit of the monks of old.

The immediate need of the nation is a large supply of skilled workmen, of men with inventive genius, and of employers alert in the development of new ideas.

There is one—and only one—way to obtain these admirable results. It is by producing workmen, men of science, and employers who enjoy their work. View the matter practically in the light of our knowledge of average human nature. Is it likely that a tired, bored workman, however skilful his hands, will produce a large output of first-class work? He will limit his production, will scamp his work, and be an adept at evading inspection; he will be slow in adapting himself to new methods; he will be a focus of discontent, full of unpractical revolutionary ideas, controlled by no sympathetic apprehension of the real working of trade conditions. If, in the troubled times which may be before us, you wish appreciably to increase the chance of some savage upheaval, introduce widespread technical education and ignore the Benedictine ideal. Society will then get what it deserves.

Again, inventive genius requires pleasurable mental activity as a condition for its vigorous exercise. "Necessity is the mother of invention" is a silly proverb. " Necessity is the mother of futile dodges " is much nearer to the truth. The basis of the growth of modern invention is science, and science is almost wholly the outgrowth of pleasurable intellectual curiosity.

The third class are the employers, who are to be enterprising. Now it is to be observed that it is the successful employers who are the important people to get at, the men with business connections all over the world, men who are already rich. No doubt there will always be a continuous process of rise and fall of businesses. But it is futile to expect flourishing trade, if in the mass the successful houses of business are suffering from atrophy. Now if these men conceive their businesses as merely indifferent means for acquiring other disconnected opportunities of life, they have no spur to alertness. They are already doing very well, the mere momentum of their present business engagements will carry them on for their time. They are not at all likely to bother themselves with the doubtful chances of new methods. Their real soul is in the other side of their life. Desire for money will produce hard-fistedness and not enterprise. There is much more hope for humanity from manufacturers who enjoy their work than from those who continue in irksome business with the object of founding hospitals.

Finally, there can be no prospect of industrial peace so long as masters and men in the mass conceive themselves as engaged in a soulless operation of extracting money from the public. Enlarged views of the work performed, and of the communal service thereby rendered, can be the only basis on which to found sympathetic co-operation.

The conclusion to be drawn from this discussion is, that alike for masters and for men a technical or technological education, which is to have any chance of satisfying the practical needs of the nation, must be conceived in a liberal spirit as a real intellectual enlightenment in regard to principles applied and services rendered. In such an education geometry and poetry are as essential as turning lathes.

The mythical figure of Plato may stand for modern liberal education as does that of St.

D

Benedict for technical education. We need not entangle ourselves in the qualifications necessary for a balanced representation of the actual thoughts of the actual men. They are used here as symbolic figures typical of antithetical notions. We consider Plato in the light of the type of culture he now inspires.

In its essence a liberal education is an education for thought and for æsthetic appreciation. It proceeds by imparting a knowledge of the master-pieces of thought, of imaginative literature, and of art. The action which it contemplates is command. It is an aristocratic education implying leisure. This Platonic ideal has rendered imperishable services to European civilisation. It has encouraged art, it has fostered that spirit of disinterested curiosity which is the origin of science, it has maintained the dignity of mind in the face of material force, a dignity which claims freedom of thought. Plato did not, like St. Benedict, bother himself to be a fellow-worker with his slaves; but he must rank among the emancipators of mankind. His type of culture is the peculiar inspiration of the liberal aristocrat, the class from which Europe derives what ordered liberty it now possesses. For centuries, from Pope Nicholas V to the schools of the Jesuits, and from the Jesuits to the modern headmasters of English public schools, this educational ideal has had the strenuous support of the clergy.

For certain people it is a very good education. It suits their type of mind and the circumstances amid which their life is passed. But more has been claimed for it than this. All education has been judged adequate or defective according to its approximation to this sole type.

The essence of the type is a large discursive knowledge of the best literature. The ideal product of the type is the man who is acquainted with the best that has been written. He will have acquired the chief languages, he will have considered the histories of the rise and fall of nations, the poetic expression of human feeling, and have read the great dramas and novels. He will also be well grounded in the chief philosophies, and have attentively read those philosophic authors who are distinguished for lucidity of style.

It is obvious that, except at the close of a long life, he will not have much time for anything else if any approximation is to be made to the fulfilment of this programme. One is reminded of the calculation in a dialogue of Lucian that, before a man could be justified in practising any one of the current ethical systems, he should have spent a hundred and fifty years in examining their credentials.

Such ideals are not for human beings. What is meant by a liberal culture is nothing so ambitious as a full acquaintance with the varied literary expression of civilised mankind from Asia to Europe, and from Europe to America. A small selection only is required; but then, as we are told, it is a selection of the very best. I have my doubts of a selection which includes Xenophon and omits Confucius, but then I have read neither in the original. The ambitious programme of a liberal education really shrinks to a study of some fragments of literature included in a couple of important languages.

But the expression of the human spirit is not confined to literature. There are the other arts, and there are the sciences. Also education must pass beyond the passive reception of the ideas of others. Powers of initiative must be strengthened. Unfortunately initiative does not mean just one acquirement—there is initiative in thought, initiative in action, and the imaginative initiative of art; and these three categories require many subdivisions.

The field of acquirement is large, and the individual so fleeting and so fragmentary: classical scholars, scientists, headmasters are alike ignoramuses.

There is a curious illusion that a more complete culture was possible when there was less to know. Surely the only gain was, that it was more possible to remain unconscious of ignorance. It cannot have been a gain to Plato to have read neither Shakespeare, nor Newton, nor Darwin. The achievements of a liberal education have in recent times not been worsened. The change is that its pretensions have been found out.

My point is, that no course of study can claim any position of ideal completeness. Nor are the omitted factors of subordinate importance. The insistence in the Platonic culture on disinterested intellectual appreciation is a psychological error. Action and our implication in the transition of events amid the evitable bond of cause to effect are fundamental. An education which strives to divorce intellectual or æsthetic life from these fundamental facts carries with it the decadence of civilisation. Essentially culture should be for action, and its effect should be to divest labour from the associations of aimless toil. Art exists that we may know the deliverances of our senses as good. It heightens the sense-world.

Disinterested scientific curiosity is a passion for an ordered intellectual vision of the connection of events. But the goal of such curiosity is the marriage of action to thought. This essential intervention of action even in abstract science is often overlooked. No man of science wants merely to know. He acquires knowledge to appease his passion for discovery. He does not discover in order to know, he knows in order to discover. The pleasure which art and science can give to toil is the enjoyment which arises from successfully directed intention. Also it is the same pleasure which is yielded to the scientist and to the artist.

The antithesis between a technical and a liberal education is fallacious. There can be no adequate technical education which is not liberal, and no liberal education which is not technical : that is, no education which does not impart both technique and intellectual vision. In simpler language, education should turn out the pupil with something he knows well and something he can do well. This intimate union of practice and theory aids both. The intellect does not work best in a vacuum. The stimulation of creative impulse requires, especially in the case of a child, the quick transition to practice. Geometry and mechanics, followed by workshop practice, gain that reality without which mathematics is verbiage.

There are three main methods which are required in a national system of education, namely, the literary curriculum, the scientific curriculum, the technical curriculum. But each of these curricula should include the other two. What I mean is, that every form of education should give the pupil a technique, a science, an assortment of general ideas, and æsthetic appreciation, and that each of these sides of his training should be illuminated by the others. Lack of time, even for the most favoured pupil, makes it impossible to develop fully each curriculum. Always there must be a dominant emphasis. The most direct æsthetic training naturally falls in the technical curriculum in those cases when the training is that requisite for some art or artistic craft. But it is of high importance in both a literary and a scientific education.

The educational method of the literary curriculum is the study of language, that is, the study of our most habitual method of conveying to others our states of mind. The technique which should be acquired is the technique of verbal expression, the science is the study of the structure of language and the analysis of the relations of language to the states of mind conveyed. Furthermore, the subtle relations of language to feeling, and the high development of the sense organs to which written and spoken words appeal, lead to keen æsthetic appreciations being aroused by the successful employment of language. Finally, the wisdom of the world is preserved in the masterpieces of linguistic composition.

This curriculum has the merit of homogeneity. All its various parts are co-ordinated and play into each other's hands. We can hardly be surprised that such a curriculum, when once broadly established, should have claimed the position of the sole perfect type of education. Its defect is unduly to emphasise the importance of language. Indeed the varied importance of verbal expression is so overwhelming that its sober estimation is difficult. Recent generations have been witnessing the retreat of literature, and of literary forms of expression, from their position of unique importance in intellectual life. In order truly to become a servant and a minister of nature something more is required than literary aptitudes.

A scientific education is primarily a training in the art of observing natural phenomena, and in the knowledge and deduction of laws concerning the sequence of such phenomena. But here, as in the case of a liberal education, we are met by the limitations imposed by shortness of time. There are many types of natural phenomena, and to each type there corresponds a science with its peculiar modes of observation, and its peculiar types of thought employed in the deduction of laws. A study of science in general is impossible in education, all that can be achieved is the study of two or three allied sciences. Hence the charge of narrow specialism urged against any education which is primarily scientific. It is obvious that the charge is apt to be well-founded; and it is worth considering how, within the limits of a scientific education and to the advantage of such an education, the danger can be avoided.

Such a discussion requires the consideration of

technical education. A technical education is in the main a training in the art of utilising knowledge for the manufacture of material products. Such a training emphasises manual skill, and the co-ordinated action of hand and eye, and judgment in the control of the process of construction. But judgment necessitates knowledge of those natural processes of which the manufacture is the utilisation. Thus somewhere in technical training an education in scientific knowledge is required. If you minimise the scientific side, you will confine it to the scientific experts; if you maximise it, you will impart it in some measure to the men, and—what is of no less importance— to the directors and managers of the businesses.

Technical education is not necessarily allied exclusively to science on its mental side. It may be an education for an artist or for apprentices to an artistic craft. In that case æsthetic appreciation will have to be cultivated in connection with it.

An evil side of the Platonic culture has been its total neglect of technical education as an ingredient in the complete development of ideal human beings. This neglect has arisen from two disastrous antitheses, namely, that between mind and body, and that between thought and action. I will here interject, solely to avoid criticism, that I am well aware that the Greeks highly valued physical beauty and physical activity. They had, however, that perverted sense of values which is the nemesis of slave-owning.

I lay it down as an educational axiom that in teaching you will come to grief as soon as you forget that your pupils have bodies. This is exactly the mistake of the post-renaissance Platonic curriculum. But nature can be kept at bay by no pitchfork; so in English education, being expelled from the classroom, she returned with a cap and bells in the form of all-conquering athleticism.

The connections between intellectual activity and the body, though diffused in every bodily feeling, are focussed in the eyes, the ears, the voice, and the hands. There is a co-ordination of senses and thought, and also a reciprocal influence between brain activity and material creative activity. In this reaction the hands are peculiarly important. It is a moot point whether the human hand created the human brain, or the brain created the hand. Certainly the connection is intimate and reciprocal. Such deep-seated relations are not widely atrophied by a few hundred years of disuse in exceptional families.

The disuse of hand-craft is a contributory cause to the brain-lethargy of aristocracies, which is only mitigated by sport where the concurrent brain-activity is reduced to a minimum and the hand-craft lacks subtlety. The necessity for constant writing and vocal exposition is some slight stimulus to the thought-power of the professional classes. Great readers, who exclude other activities, are not distinguished by subtlety of brain. They tend to be timid conventional thinkers. No doubt this is partly due to their excessive knowledge outrunning their powers of thought; but it is partly due to the lack of brain-stimulus from the productive activities of hand or voice.

In estimating the importance of technical education we must rise above the exclusive association of learning with book-learning. First-hand knowledge is the ultimate basis of intellectual life. To a large extent book-learning conveys second-hand information, and as such can never rise to the importance of immediate practice. Our goal is to see the immediate event of our lives as instances of our general ideas. What the learned world tends to offer is one second-hand scrap of information illustrating ideas derived from another second-hand scrap of information. The second-handedness of the learned world is the secret of its mediocrity. It is tame because it has never been scared by facts. The main importance of Francis Bacon's influence does not lie in any peculiar theory of inductive reasoning which he happened to express, but in the revolt against second-hand information of which he was a leader.

The peculiar merit of a scientific education should be, that it bases thought upon first-hand observation; and the corresponding merit of a technical education is, that it follows our deep natural instinct to translate thought into manual skill, and manual activity into thought.

We are a Mathematical Association, and it is natural to ask: Where do we come in? We come in just at this point.

The thought which science evokes is logical thought. Now logic is of two kinds: the logic of discovery and the logic of the discovered.

The logic of discovery consists in the weighing of probabilities, in discarding details deemed to be irrelevant, in divining the general rules according to which events occur, and in testing hypotheses by devising suitable experiments. This is inductive logic.

The logic of the discovered is the deduction of the special events which, under certain circumstances, would happen in obedience to the assumed laws of nature. Thus when the laws are discovered or assumed, their utilisation entirely depends on deductive logic. Without deductive logic science would be entirely useless. It is merely a barren game to ascend from the particular to the general, unless afterwards we can reverse the process and descend from the general to the particular, ascending and descending like the angels on Jacob's ladder. When Newton had divined the law of gravitation he at once proceeded to calculate the earth's attractions on an apple at its surface and on the moon. We may note in passing that inductive logic would be impossible without deductive logic. Thus Newton's calculations were an essential step in his inductive verification of the great law.

Now mathematics is nothing else than the more complicated parts of the art of deductive reasoning, especially where it concerns number, quantity, and space.

In the teaching of science, the art of thought should be taught : namely, the art of forming clear conceptions applying to first-hand experience, the art of divining the general truths which apply, the art of testing divinations, and the art of utilising general truths by reasoning to more particular cases of some peculiar importance. Furthermore, a power of scientific exposition is necessary, so that the relevant issues from a confused mass of ideas can be stated clearly, with due emphasis on important points.

By the time a science, or a small group of sciences, has been taught thus amply, with due regard to the general art of thought, we have gone a long way towards correcting the specialism of science. The worst of a scientific education based, as necessarily must be the case, on one or two particular branches of science, is that the teachers under the influence of the examination system are apt merely to stuff their pupils with the narrow results of these special sciences. It is essential that the generality of the method be continually brought to light and contrasted with the speciality of the particular application. A man who only knows his own science, as a routine peculiar to that science, does not even know that. He has no fertility of thought, no power of quickly seizing the bearing of alien ideas. He will discover nothing, and be stupid in practical applications.

This exhibition of the general in the particular is extremely difficult to effect, especially in the case of younger pupils. The art of education is never easy. To surmount its difficulties, especially those of elementary education, is a task worthy of the highest genius. It is the training of human souls.

Mathematics, well taught, should be the most powerful instrument in gradually implanting this generality of idea. The essence of mathematics is perpetually to be discarding more special ideas in favour of more general ideas, and special methods in favour of general methods. We express the conditions of a special problem in the form of an equation, but that equation will serve for a hundred other problems, scattered through diverse sciences. The general reasoning is always the powerful reasoning, because deductive cogency is the property of abstract form.

Here, again, we must be careful. We shall ruin mathematical education if we use it merely to impress general truths. The general ideas are the means of connecting particular results. After all, it is the concrete special cases which are important. Thus in the handling of mathematics in your results you cannot be too concrete, and in your methods you cannot be too general. The essential course of reasoning is to generalise what is particular, and then to particularise what is general. Without generality there is no reasoning, without concreteness there is no importance.

Concreteness is the strength of technical education. I would remind you that truths which lack the highest generality are not necessarily concrete facts. For example, $x + y = y + x$ is an algebraic truth more general than $2 + 2 = 4$. But " two and two make four " is itself a highly general proposition lacking any element of concreteness. To obtain a concrete proposition immediate intuition of a truth concerning particular objects is requisite; for example, " these two apples and those apples together make four apples " is a concrete proposition, if you have direct perception or immediate memory of the apples.

In order to obtain the full realisation of truths as applying, and not as empty formulæ, there is no alternative to technical education. Mere

passive observation is not sufficient. In creation only is there vivid insight into the properties
of the object thereby produced. If you want
to understand anything, make it yourself, is a
sound rule. Your faculties will be alive, your
thoughts gain vividness by an immediate translation into acts. Your ideas gain that reality which
comes from seeing the limits of their application.

In elementary education this doctrine has
long been put into practice. Young children are
taught to familiarise themselves with shapes and
colours by simple manual operations of cutting
out and of sorting. But good though this is,
it is not quite what I mean. That is practical
experience before you think, experience antecedent to thought in order to create ideas, a
very excellent discipline. But technical education should be much more than that : it is creative experience while you think, experience
which realises your thought, experience which
teaches you to co-ordinate act and thought,
experience leading you to associate thought
with foresight and foresight with achievement.
Technical education gives theory, and a shrewd
insight as to where theory fails.

A technical education is not to be conceived
as a maimed alternative to the perfect Platonic
culture : namely, as a defective training unfortunately made necessary by cramped conditions
of life. No human being can attain to anything

but fragmentary knowledge and a fragmentary training of his capacities. There are, however, three main roads along which we can proceed with good hope of advancing towards the best balance of intellect and character: these are the way of literary culture, the way of scientific culture, the way of technical culture. No one of these methods can be exclusively followed without grave loss of intellectual activity and of character. But a mere mechanical mixture of the three curricula will produce bad results in the shape of scraps of information never interconnected or utilised. We have already noted as one of the strong points of the traditional literary culture that all its parts are co-ordinated. The problem of education is to retain the dominant emphasis, whether literary, scientific, or technical, and without loss of co-ordination to infuse into each way of education something of the other two.

To make definite the problem of technical education fix attention on two ages: one thirteen, when elementary education ends; and the other seventeen, when technical education ends so far as it is compressed within a school curriculum. I am aware that for artisans in junior technical schools a three-years' course would be more usual. On the other hand, for naval officers, and for directing classes generally, a longer time can be afforded. We want to consider the

E

principles to govern a curriculum which shall land these children at the age of seventeen in the position of having technical skill useful to the community.

Their technical manual training should start at thirteen, bearing a modest proportion to the rest of their work, and should increase in each year finally to attain to a substantial proportion. Above all things it should not be too specialised. Workshop finish and workshop dodges, adapted to one particular job, should be taught in the commercial workshop, and should form no essential part of the school course. A properly trained worker would pick them up in no time. In all education the main cause of failure is staleness. Technical education is doomed if we conceive it as a system for catching children young and for giving them one highly specialised manual aptitude. The nation has need of a fluidity of labour, not merely from place to place, but also within reasonable limits of allied aptitudes, from one special type of work to another special type. I know that here I am on delicate ground, and I am not claiming that men while they are specialising on one sort of work should spasmodically be set to other kinds. That is a question of trade organisation with which educationalists have no concern. I am only asserting the principles that training should be broader than the ultimate specialisation, and that the resulting power of adaptation to varying demands is advantageous to the workers, to the employers, and to the nation.

In considering the intellectual side of the curriculum we must be guided by the principle of the co-ordination of studies. In general, the intellectual studies most immediately related to manual training will be some branches of science. More than one branch will, in fact, be concerned; and even if that be not the case, it is impossible to narrow down scientific study to a single thin line of thought. It is possible, however, provided that we do not press the classification too far, roughly to classify technical pursuits according to the dominant science involved. We thus find a sixfold division, namely, (1) Geometrical techniques, (2) Mechanical techniques, (3) Physical techniques, (4) Chemical techniques, (5) Biological techniques, (6) Techniques of commerce and of social service.

By this division, it is meant that apart from auxiliary sciences some particular science requires emphasis in the training for most occupations. We can, for example, reckon carpentry, ironmongery, and many artistic crafts among geometrical techniques. Similarly agriculture is a biological technique. Probably cookery, if it includes food catering, would fall midway between biological, physical, and chemical sciences, though of this I am not sure.

The sciences associated with commerce and social service would be partly algebra, including arithmetic and statistics, and partly geography and history. But this section is somewhat heterogeneous in its scientific affinities. Anyhow the exact way in which technical pursuits are classified in relation to science is a detail. The essential point is, that with some thought it is possible to find scientific courses which illuminate most occupations. Furthermore, the problem is well understood, and has been brilliantly solved in many of the schools of technology and junior technical schools throughout the country.

In passing from science to literature, in our review of the intellectual elements of technical education, we note that many studies hover between the two : for example, history and geography. They are both of them very essential in education, provided that they are the right history and the right geography. Also books giving descriptive accounts of general results, and trains of thought in various sciences fall in the same category. Such books should be partly historical and partly expository of the main ideas which have finally arisen. Prof. R. A. Gregory's recent book, *Discovery*, and the *Home University Library* series illustrate my meaning. Their value in education depends on their quality as mental stimulants. They must not be inflated with gas on the wonders of science, and must be informed with a broad outlook.

It is unfortunate that the literary element in education has rarely been considered apart from grammatical study. The historical reason is, that when the modern Platonic curriculum was being formed Latin and Greek were the sole keys which rendered great literature accessible. But there is no necessary connection between literature and grammar. The great age of Greek literature was already past before the arrival of the grammarians of Alexandria. Of all types of men to-day existing, classical scholars are the most remote from the Greeks of the Periclean times.

Mere literary knowledge is of slight importance. The only thing that matters is, how it is known. The facts related are nothing. Literature only exists to express and develop that imaginative world which is our life, the kingdom which is within us. It follows that the literary side of a technical education should consist in an effort to make the pupils enjoy literature. It does not matter what they know, but the enjoyment is vital. The great English Universities, under whose direct authority school-children are examined in plays of Shakespeare, to the certain destruction of their enjoyment, should be prosecuted for soul-murder.

Now there are two kinds of intellectual

enjoyment : the enjoyment of creation, and the enjoyment of relaxation. They are not necessarily separated. A change of occupation may give the full tide of happiness which comes from the concurrence of both forms of pleasure. The appreciation of literature is really creation. The written word, its music, and its associations, are only the stimuli. The vision which they evoke is our own doing. No one, no genius other than our own, can make our own life live. But except for those engaged in literary occupations, literature is also a relaxation. It gives exercise to that other side which any occupation must suppress during the working hours. Art also has the same function in life as has literature.

To obtain the pleasure of relaxation requires no help. The pleasure is merely to cease doing. Some such pure relaxation is a necessary condition of health. Its dangers are notorious, and to the greater part of the necessary relaxation nature has affixed, not enjoyment, but the oblivion of sleep. Creative enjoyment is the outcome of successful effort and requires help for its initiation. Such enjoyment is necessary for high-speed work and for original achievement.

To speed up production with unrefreshed workmen is a disastrous economic policy. Temporary success will be at the expense of the nation, which, for long years of their lives, will have to support worn-out artisans—unemployables.

Equally disastrous is the alternation of spasms of effort with periods of pure relaxation. Such periods are the seed-times of degeneration, unless rigorously curtailed. The normal recreation should be change of activity, satisfying the cravings of instincts. Games afford such activity. Their disconnection emphasises the relaxation, but their excess leaves us empty.

It is here that literature and art should play an essential part in a healthily organised nation. Their services to economic production would be only second to those of sleep or of food. I am not now talking of the training of an artist, but of the use of art as a condition of healthy life. It is analogous to sunshine in the physical world.

When we have once rid our minds of the idea that knowledge is to be exacted, there is no especial difficulty or expense involved in helping the growth of artistic enjoyment. All school-children could be sent at regular intervals to neighbouring theatres where suitable plays could be subsidised. Similarly for concerts and cinema films. Pictures are more doubtful in their popular attraction; but interesting representations of scenes or ideas which the children have read about would probably appeal. The pupils themselves should be encouraged in artistic efforts. Above all the art of reading aloud should be cultivated. The Roger de Coverley essays of Addison are perfect examples of readable prose.

Art and literature have not merely an indirect effect on the main energies of life. Directly, they give vision. The world spreads wide beyond the deliverances of material sense, with subtleties of reaction and with pulses of emotion. Vision is the necessary antecedent to control and to direction. In the contest of races which in its final issues will be decided in the workshops and not on the battle-field, the victory will belong to those who are masters of stores of trained nervous energy, working under conditions favourable to growth. One such essential condition is Art.

If there had been time, there are other things which I should like to have said : for example, to advocate the inclusion of one foreign language in all education. From direct observation I know this to be possible for artisan children. But enough has been put before you, to make plain the principles with which we should undertake national education.

In conclusion, I recur to the thought of the Benedictines, who saved for mankind the vanishing civilisation of the ancient world by linking together knowledge, labour, and moral energy. Our danger is to conceive practical affairs as the kingdom of evil, in which success is only possible by the extrusion of ideal aims. I believe that such a conception is a fallacy directly negatived by practical experience. In education this error takes the form of a mean view of technical training. Our forefathers in the dark ages saved themselves by embodying high ideals in great organisations. It is our task, without servile imitation, boldly to exercise our creative energies, remembering amid discouragements that the coldest hour immediately precedes the dawn.

CHAPTER III

*Address at the Prize Distribution, Borough
Polytechnic Institute, Southwark,
16th February, 1917*

I WILL commence by drawing your attention
to some of the satisfactory features of the Principal's report on the work of the Institute during
the past year. It has been a year of great difficulties. Some of our staff are serving with the
colours, and our classes have been depleted.
But in spite of everything, we have done very
well. First, the average result in the examinations has been good, surprisingly good in view
of the present circumstances. The Governors
attach great importance to the maintenance of
a high average result; it is the best single test
of efficiency. Again, our individual successes
have been notable. We have gained—I say *we*
because we are all one in our pleasure at these
successes—we have gained two £80 L.C.C. scholarships, nineteen exhibitions, in addition to a first-
place, and medals, prizes and certificates. All
this is very satisfactory. It tells of efficient

58

teaching, and of hard work and regular attendance on the part of the students. We know that we are keeping up the standard of efficiency which in the past has been a source of pride to every one connected with this Institute.

Now all this good work does not come about by itself without any one making an effort. Such a record requires our skilled staff of teachers and organisers. They have worked very hard during the last session under great difficulties, in order to create the successful result which we are here to celebrate. I know something about teaching. It is very exacting work, and can be made successful only by continual devotion. I am sure that I am voicing your feelings, and I know that I am expressing those of the Governors, when I thank the ladies and gentlemen of the staff very heartily for their services during the last session.

Prize-givings are always pleasant occasions. We have come here to think about our successes, and to congratulate our students. There is no more satisfactory Governors' Meeting in the course of the year than when we meet on this occasion, and face our friends and tell them how pleased we are at the successful result of their hard work. This evening I am in a doubly happy position, for my colleagues have asked me to be their spokesman in tendering our good wishes to the prize-winners. You have worked hard and you have done well, and I am sure that you all deserve your successes; they are a pleasure not only to you, but in your homes and to your companions and fellow-students.

Successful work here will enable you to acquire skill in your trades, and thereby the better to earn your living. Earning a living is on the average no bad test of service rendered to the community. A man who has made himself skilful in his trade and has done well for himself in his walk of life, has in general good reason to believe that he is a citizen who has benefited his country. It is an evil day for a nation when it loses respect for success in industry.

But if you steer your lives by the compass which points steadily to the North Pole of personal success, you will have missed your greatest chances in life. The genial climate is in the south.

What I mean is this : you must make up your mind to find the best part of your happiness in kindly helpful relations with others. It should be our ambition to leave our own small corner of the world a little tidier and a little happier than when we entered it. I am well aware that this is an old story; but old stories are sometimes true, and this is the biggest truth in the whole world. The warm kindly feelings are the happy feelings. The fortunate people are those whose minds are filled with thoughts in which they forget themselves and remember others. It is not true that nature is a mere scene of struggle in which every one competes with his neighbour. Those communities thrive best and last longest which are filled with a spirit of mutual help.

The future of the country lies with you. The crown of your success is the promise of future work, often unrecognised work, done under discouragement, but done steadily and cheerfully. It is on you that the country depends for the maintenance and the growth of those ideals without which a race withers. Do not be discouraged by difficulties which seem unsurmountable. The conditions of life which mould us all are modified by our will, by our energy, and by the purity of our intentions.

If we may judge of intensity of feeling by length of memory, the enjoyment of receiving a prize bites very deep. Across the space of more than forty years, before many of your parents were born, or when they were being carried about in long clothes, I can remember, as if it were yesterday, the occasion when I received my first prize at school. I can see the mediæval schoolroom, the headmaster, and my companions. Perhaps some of you, when a generation has passed by, will remember the scene to-night—this Stanley Gymnasium recalling the memory of Miss Maude Stanley, who devoted to our welfare so much of her energy and her thought—the adjoining Edric Hall associated with the name of

Mr. Edric Bayley, the Father of the Institute; Mr. Millis and Miss Smith, the first Principal and the first Lady Superintendent, the architects of our prosperity; Mr. Leonard Spicer, our Chairman and member of a family and of a firm known throughout the world, and respected in proportion as they are known. And the cause why tonight we are a small gathering is one more reason why this assembly can never slip from your memory. We meet at a moment when England stands in as deadly a peril as in any previous moment of her history—such peril as when the Spanish ships of the Armada rode in the English Channel, or when Napoleon watched our coast across the Strait of Dover. The present danger can be overcome only by the same courage as that which saved our freedom in those former times.

Therefore, to-night, in recalling the activities of the various sections of our society which form this great Polytechnic Institute, our thoughts go further afield. They travel by land and by sea, till they bring before our minds the gallant band whom this Institute has sent to the Front —more than 800 of our members are with the Colours. What our fighting men have done for us, for the world in general, and for the future of England, is so overwhelming that words cannot praise them enough. I will just say one thing to you: When you read of great deeds

done in past times, of perils encountered, of
adventures, of undaunted courage, of patriotism,
of self-sacrifice, of suffering endured for noble
cause, you each can say—I, too, have known such
heroes; they are among my countrymen, they are
among my fellow-workers, they are among my
fellow-students and companions, they are among
the dear inmates of my home. And for those
who have fallen, it is for us to erect a monument
sufficient to transmit to future ages the memory
of their sacrifice. For this purpose there is only
one memorial which can suffice, namely, the
cause for which they died. The greatness of
England, the future of England, has been left
by them to our keeping. Guard it well.

The greatness of a country is nothing else than
the greatness of the lives of the men and of the
women who compose it. Do not look round and
think who ought to be great Englishmen—be
great yourselves—you are the people to achieve it,
you who are sitting here to-night. There can
be no substitute service for this purpose. It is
the collective energy of the whole people that will
be needed to fashion a new England worthy of
the sufferings which for its sake have been
endured.

A few days ago I asked a man who has worked
in Egypt for many years under Lord Kitchener,
what he would pick out as the best sign of Lord
Kitchener's greatness. He answered, whatever

Kitchener set himself to do, thereby became important. Now that is the secret of it all— take hold of your opportunities and make them important.

Here we are in this Borough Polytechnic. What an opportunity it represents. This Institute is a centre for social meeting, a centre for recreation, a centre for education, a centre for discussion. We will not sacrifice any one of our sides. They must all be part of the greatness which we claim. Make them all first-rate.

Consider first the social and recreative sides. For heaven's sake don't think that you must be dull in order to be great. There is no finer test of a nation than the way in which it fashions its amusements. Three centuries ago after the Armada we made a good start in Southwark. Shakespeare had his theatre here and wrote his plays to be acted in this borough. He has walked these streets, and if you had met him in Westminster he would, quite likely, have told you that he was going down to the " Elephant." And even now the performances given at the " Old Vic " are among the best in London for the purpose of seeing his plays properly acted. What Southwark has done for the drama, she can do for the other arts, by using this Institute as the instrument for her energies. Why should we not be a centre for artistic enterprise—I mean for our own art and our own enterprise, thought of by ourselves and enjoyed by ourselves and carried through by ourselves ? We shall not always enjoy each others' creations, but the great point is to make our own efforts. Of course all efforts require preparation and stimulus and knowledge of what others are doing.

At the present time—interrupted for the moment by the war—a great revolution in the art of painting is in progress throughout the world. Its centres are Paris and Italy and London and Munich, and its origin in the far east, in China and Japan. There are two sides as in every revolution, the Conservatives and the Revolutionists. Our own frescoes in a neighbouring room represent an early stage of the movement in London. Why should we not know all about it—obtain loans of pictures which illustrate its phases and its cross currents, and compare these with examples of the old style ?

But pictures are only one phase of art, and not the sort of art which we ourselves can produce most easily. There are music, dancing, recitation, literature, carving and modelling, and the various decorative arts, such as embroidery, bookbinding, dress-making and upholstery. This list, incomplete as it is, tells us two great truths —you cannot separate art and recreation, and you cannot separate art and business. The list includes items which we consider as amusements, and items which we think of as business. We

F

began with dancing and ended with upholstery. Make them all beautiful.

Beautiful things have dignity. Enjoy the rhythm of your dancing and admire the beauty of your embroidery or your bookbinding. In whatever you do, have an ideal of excellence. Any separation between art and work is not only an error, but it is very bad business. Our brave allies, the French, have made Paris the art centre of the world. They have built up and maintain their large and lucrative trade in the decorative products of France, mainly by reason of three qualities which they possess. In the first place, they enjoy art themselves, and reverence it. In the second place, they have a tremendous power of hard work. And in the third place, every Frenchman, and still more every French-woman, have within them an immense fund of common sense. The threefold secret is, Love of Art, Industry, and Common Sense.

To make available our industry and common sense in the trades where they are wanted, rigorous training in schools of design and technique are necessary. We have such departments here. But all such training of you will be a failure unless you yourselves enjoy art and beauty as a natural recreation. A technical school of training is like a deep, narrow well, sunk with careful labour to tap the underground river of water which flows below the surface of our natures.

But your well will be dry unless the bright warm sun has first drawn up the vapour from the wide ocean, and the free untrammelled breezes have carried the clouds hither and thither, until at length they break as it were by chance over the distant hills and soak the land with their downpour.

What I have said about art is a parable which applies to other occupations and other studies. It is more than a parable; it is the literal truth. The love of art is the love of excellence, it is the enjoyment of the triumph of design over the shapeless products of chance forces. An engineer, who is worth his salt, loves the beauty of his machines, shown in their adjustment of parts and in their swift, smooth motions. He loves also the sense of foresight and of insight which knowledge can give him. People say that machinery and commerce are driving beauty out of the modern world. I do not believe it. A new beauty is being added, a more intellectual beauty, appealing to the understanding as much as to the eye.

The wonder of London ever takes the mind with fresh astonishment. The city possesses parks, and palaces, and cathedrals. But no other parts of it surpass in wonder its houses of business and its workshops and its factories.

In the next few years the future of the world will be decided for centuries to come. The battles of this war are only the first part of the contest between races, and between the ways of life for which those races stand. We believe that England, with its various peoples and communities scattered in islands and continents beyond the seas, stands for ways of life infinitely precious, the way of humanity, the way of liberty, the way of self-government, the way of good order based on toleration and kindly feeling, the way of peaceful industry. The final decision in this struggle will be found in the workshops of the world. It lies in your hands. Statesmen and emperors will only register the results which you have achieved. Your weapons will be skill, and energy, and knowledge. You will require a sane understanding of your own rights, and a sane understanding of the rights and the difficulties of other classes. The greatness of England will be your greatness, and its success your success.

The arsenal for war is at Woolwich. This Polytechnic Institute is an arsenal for peace, where you can find the weapons for the conquest of your lives.

CHAPTER IV

THE MATHEMATICAL CURRICULUM

(Presidential Address to the London Branch of the Mathematical Association, 1912)

THE situation in regard to education at the present time cannot find its parallel without going back for some centuries to the break-up of the mediæval traditions of learning. Then, as now, the traditional intellectual outlook, despite the authority which it had justly acquired from its notable triumphs, had grown to be too narrow for the interests of mankind. The result of this shifting of human interest was a demand for a parallel shifting of the basis of education, so as to fit the pupils for the ideas which later in life would in fact occupy their minds. Any serious fundamental change in the intellectual outlook of human society must necessarily be followed by an educational revolution. It may be delayed for a generation by vested interests or by the passionate attachment of some leaders of thought to the cycle of ideas within which they received their own mental stimulus at an impressionable age. But the law is inexorable that education to be living and effective must be directed to informing pupils with those ideas, and to creating for them those capacities which will enable them to appreciate the current thought of their epoch.

There is no such thing as a successful system of education in a vacuum, that is to say, a system which is divorced from immediate contact with the existing intellectual atmosphere. Education which is not modern shares the fate of all organic things which are kept too long.

But the blessed word " modern " does not really solve our difficulties. What we mean is, relevant to modern thought, either in the ideas imparted or in the aptitudes produced. Something found out only yesterday may not really be modern in this sense. It may belong to some bygone system of thought prevalent in a previous age, or, what is very much more likely, it may be too recondite. When we demand that education should be relevant to modern thought, we are referring to thoughts broadly spread throughout cultivated society. It is this question of the unfitness of recondite subjects for use in general education which I wish to make the keynote of my address this afternoon.

It is in fact rather a delicate subject for us mathematicians. Outsiders are apt to accuse our subject of being recondite. Let us grasp the nettle at once and frankly admit that in general opinion it is the very typical example of reconditeness. By this word I do not mean difficulty, but that the ideas involved are of highly special application, and rarely influence thought.

This liability to reconditeness is the characteristic evil which is apt to destroy the utility of mathematics in liberal education. So far as it clings to the educational use of the subject, so far we must acquiesce in a miserably low level of mathematical attainment among cultivated people in general. I yield to no one in my anxiety to increase the educational scope of mathematics. The way to achieve this end is not by a mere blind demand for more mathematics. We must face the real difficulty which obstructs its extended use.

Is the subject recondite? Now, viewed as a whole, I think it is. *Securus judicat orbis terrarum*—the general judgment of mankind is sure.

The subject as it exists in the minds and in the books of students of mathematics *is* recondite. It proceeds by deducing innumerable special results from general ideas, each result more recondite than the preceding. It is not my task this afternoon to defend mathematics as a subject for profound study. It can very well take care of itself. What I want to emphasise is, that the very reasons which make this science a delight to its students are reasons which obstruct its use as an educational instrument—namely, the boundless wealth of deductions from the interplay of general theorems, their complication, their apparent remoteness from the ideas from which the argument started, the variety of methods, and their purely abstract character which brings, as its gift, eternal truth.

Of course, all these characteristics are of priceless value to students; for ages they have fascinated some of the keenest intellects. My only remark is that, except for a highly selected class, they are fatal in education. The pupils are bewildered by a multiplicity of detail, without apparent relevance either to great ideas or to ordinary thoughts. The extension of this sort of training in the direction of acquiring more detail is the last measure to be desired in the interests of education.

The conclusion at which we arrive is, that mathematics, if it is to be used in general education, must be subjected to a rigorous process of selection and adaptation. I do not mean, what is of course obvious, that however much time we devote to the subject the average pupil will not get very far. But that, however limited the progress, certain characteristics of the subject, natural at any stage, must be rigorously excluded. The science as presented to young pupils must lose its aspect of reconditeness. It must, on the face of it, deal directly and simply with a few general ideas of far-reaching importance.

Now, in this matter of the reform of mathematical instruction, the present generation of teachers may take a very legitimate pride in its achievements. It has shown immense energy in reform, and has accomplished more than would have been thought possible in so short a time. It is not always recognised how difficult is the task of changing a well-established curriculum entrenched behind public examinations.

But for all that, great progress has been made, and, to put the matter at its lowest, the old dead tradition has been broken up. I want to indicate this afternoon the guiding idea which should direct our efforts at reconstruction. I have already summed it up in a phrase, namely, we must aim at the elimination of reconditeness from the educational use of the subject.

Our courses of instruction should be planned to illustrate simply a succession of ideas of obvious importance. All pretty divagations should be rigorously excluded. The goal to be aimed at is that the pupil should acquire familiarity with abstract thought, should realise how it applies to particular concrete circumstances, and should know how to apply general methods to its logical investigation. With this educational ideal nothing can be worse than the aimless accretion of theorems in our text-books, which acquire their position merely because the children can be made to learn them and examiners can set neat questions on them. The bookwork to be learnt should all be very important as illustrating ideas. The examples set—and let there be as many examples as teachers find necessary —should be direct illustrations of the theorems, either by way of abstract particular cases or by way of application to concrete phenomena. Here it is worth remarking that it is quite useless to simplify the bookwork, if the examples set in examinations in fact require an extended knowledge of recondite details. There is a mistaken idea that problems test ability and genius, and that bookwork tests cram. This is not my experience. Only boys who have been specially crammed for scholarships can ever do a problem paper successfully. Bookwork properly set, not in mere snippets according to the usual bad plan, is a far better test of ability, provided that it is supplemented by direct examples. But this is a digression on the bad influence of examinations on teaching.

The main ideas which lie at the base of mathematics are not at all recondite. They are abstract. But one of the main objects of the inclusion of mathematics in a liberal education is to train the pupils to handle abstract ideas.

The science constitutes the first large group of abstract ideas which naturally occur to the mind in any precise form. For the purposes of education, mathematics consists of the relations of number, the relations of quantity, and the relations of space. This is not a general definition of mathematics, which, in my opinion, is a much more general science. But we are now discussing the use of mathematics in education. These three groups of relations, concerning number, quantity, and space, are interconnected.

Now, in education we proceed from the particular to the general. Accordingly, children should be taught the use of these ideas by practice among simple examples. My point is this : The goal should be, not an aimless accumulation of special mathematical theorems, but the final recognition that the preceding years of work have illustrated those relations of number, and of quantity, and of space, which are of fundamental importance. Such a training should lie at the base of all philosophical thought. In fact elementary mathematics rightly conceived would give just that philosophical discipline of which the ordinary mind is capable. But what at all costs we ought to avoid, is the pointless accumulation of details. As many examples as you like; let the children work at them for terms, or for years. But these examples should be direct illustrations of the main ideas. In this way, and this only, can the fatal reconditeness be avoided.

I am not now speaking in particular of those who are to be professional mathematicians, or of those who for professional reasons require a knowledge of certain mathematical details. We are considering the liberal education of all students, including these two classes. This general use of mathematics should be the simple study of a few general truths, well illustrated by practical examples. This study should be conceived by itself, and completely separated in idea from the professional study mentioned above, for which it would make a most excellent preparation. Its final stage should be the recognition of the general truths which the work done has illustrated. As far as I can make out, at present the final stage is the proof of some property of circles connected with triangles. Such properties are immensely interesting to mathematicians. But are they not rather recondite, and what is the precise relation of such theorems to the ideal of a liberal education? The end of all the grammatical studies of the student in classics is to read Virgil and Horace—the greatest thoughts of the greatest men. Are we content, when pleading for the adequate representation in education of our own science, to say that the end of a mathematical training is that the student should know the properties of the nine-point circle ? I ask you frankly, is it not rather a " come down " ?

This generation of mathematical teachers has done so much strenuous work in the way of reorganising mathematical instruction that there is no need to despair of its being able to elaborate a curriculum which shall leave in the minds of the pupils something even nobler than " the ambiguous case."

Let us think how this final review, closing the elementary course, might be conducted for the more intelligent pupils. Partly no doubt it requires a general oversight of the whole work done, considered without undue detail so as to emphasise the general ideas used, and their possibilities of importance when subjected to further study. Also the analytical and geo-metrical ideas find immediate application in the physical laboratory where a course of simple experimental mechanics should have been worked through. Here the point of view is twofold, the physical ideas and the mathematical ideas illustrate each other.

The mathematical ideas are essential to the precise formulation of the mechanical laws. The idea of a precise law of nature, the extent to which such laws are in fact verified in our experience, and the role of abstract thought in their formulation, then become practically appa-rent to the pupil. The whole topic of course requires detailed development with full particular illustration, and is not suggested as requiring merely a few bare abstract statements.

It would, however, be a grave error to put too much emphasis on the mere process of direct explanation of the previous work by way of final review. My point is, that the latter end of the course should be so selected that in fact the general ideas underlying all the previous mathematical work should be brought into prominence. This may well be done by apparently entering on a new subject. For example, the ideas of quantity and the ideas of number are fundamental to all precise thought. In the previous stages they will not have been sharply separated; and children are, rightly enough, pushed on to algebra without too much bother and quantity. But the more intelligent among them at the end of their curriculum would gain immensely by a careful consideration of those fundamental properties of quantity in general which lead to the introduction of numerical measurement. This is a topic which also has the advantage that the necessary books are actually to hand. Euclid's fifth book is regarded by those qualified to judge as one of the triumphs of Greek mathematics. It deals with this very point. Nothing can be more characteristic of the hopelessly illiberal character of the traditional mathematical education than the fact that this

book has always been omitted. It deals with
ideas, and therefore was ostracised. Of course
a careful selection of the more important propositions and a careful revision of the argument
are required. This also is to hand in the pub-
lications of my immediate predecessor in the
office of president, Prof. Hill. Furthermore, in
Sir T. L. Heath's complete edition of Euclid,
there is a full commentary embodying most of
what has been said and thought on the point.
Thus it is perfectly easy for teachers to inform
themselves generally on the topic. The whole
book would not be wanted, but just the few
propositions which embody the fundamental
ideas. The subject is not fit for backward
pupils; but certainly it could be made interesting to the more advanced class. There would
be great scope for interesting discussion as to
the nature of quantity, and the tests which we
should apply to ascertain when we are dealing
with quantities. The work would not be at all
in the air, but would be illustrated at every
stage by reference to actual examples of cases
where the quantitative character is absent, or
obscure, or doubtful, or evident. Temperature,
heat, electricity, pleasure and pain, mass and
distance could all be considered.

Another idea which requires illustration is
that of functionality. A function in analysis is
the counterpart of a law in the physical universe,

and of a curve in geometry. Children have studied the relations of functions to curves from the first beginning of their study of algebra, namely in drawing graphs. Of recent years there has been a great reform in respect to graphs. But at its present stage it has either gone too far or not far enough. It is not enough merely to draw a graph. The idea behind the graph—like the man behind the gun—is essential in order to make it effective. At present there is some tendency merely to set the children to draw curves, and there to leave the whole question.

In the study of simple algebraic functions and and of trigonometrical functions we are initiating the study of the precise expression of physical laws. Curves are another way of representing these laws. The simple fundamental laws—such as the inverse square and the direct distance—should be passed under review, and the applications of the simple functions to express important concrete cases of physical laws considered. I cannot help thinking that the final review of this topic might well take the form of a study of some of the main ideas of the differential calculus applied to simple curves. There is nothing particularly difficult about the conception of a rate of change; and the differentiation of a few powers of x, such as x^2, x^3, etc., could easily be effected; perhaps by the aid of geometry even sin x and cos x could be differentiated. If we once abandon our fatal habit of cramming the children with theorems which they do not understand, and will never use, there will be plenty of time to concentrate their attention on really important topics. We can give them familiarity with conceptions which really influence thought.

Before leaving this topic of physical laws and mathematical functions, there are other points to be noticed. The fact that the precise law is never really verified by observation in its full precision is capable of easy illustration and of affording excellent examples. Again, statistical laws, namely laws which are only satisfied on the average by large numbers, can easily be studied and illustrated. In fact a slight study of statistical methods and their application to social phenomena affords one of the simplest examples of the application of algebraic ideas.

Another way in which the students' ideas can be generalised is by the use of the History of Mathematics, conceived not as a mere assemblage of the dates and names of men, but as an exposition of the general current of thought which occasioned the subjects to be objects of interest at the time of their first elaboration. The use of the History of Mathematics is to be considered at a later stage of our proceedings this afternoon. Accordingly I merely draw attention

G

to it now, to point out that perhaps it is the very subject which may best obtain the results for which I am pleading.

We have indicated two main topics, namely general ideas of quantity and of laws of nature, which should be an object of study in the mathematical curriculum of a liberal education. But there is another side to mathematics which must not be overlooked. It is the chief instrument for discipline in logical method.

Now, what is logical method, and how can any one be trained in it?

Logical method is more than the mere knowledge of valid types of reasoning and practice in the concentration of mind necessary to follow them. If it were only this, it would still be very important; for the human mind was not evolved in the bygone ages for the sake of reasoning, but merely to enable mankind with more art to hunt between meals for fresh food supplies. Accordingly few people can follow close reasoning without considerable practice.

More than this is wanted to make a good reasoner, or even to enlighten ordinary people with knowledge of what constitutes the essence of the art. The art of reasoning consists in getting hold of the subject at the right end, of seizing on the few general ideas which illuminate the whole, and of persistently marshalling all subsidiary facts round them. Nobody can be a good reasoner unless by constant practice he has realised the importance of getting hold of the big ideas and of hanging on to them like grim death. For this sort of training geometry is, I think, better than algebra. The field of thought of algebra is rather obscure, whereas space is an obvious insistent thing evident to all. Then the process of simplification, or abstraction, by which all irrelevant properties of matter, such as colour, taste, and weight, are put aside is an education in itself. Again, the definitions and the propositions assumed without proof illustrate the necessity of forming clear notions of the fundamental facts of the subject-matter and of the relations between them. All this belongs to the mere prolegomena of the subject. When we come to its development, its excellence increases. The learner is not initially confronted with any symbolism which bothers the memory by its rules, however simple they may be. Also, from the very beginning the reasoning, if properly conducted, is dominated by well-marked ideas which guide each stage of development. Accordingly the essence of logical method receives immediate exemplification.

Let us now put aside for the moment the limitations introduced by the dullness of average pupils and the pressure on time due to other subjects, and consider what geometry has to offer in the way of a liberal education. I will indicate some stages in the subject, without meaning that necessarily they are to be studied in this exclusive order. The first stage is the study of *congruence*. Our perception of congruence is in practice dependent on our judgments of the invariability of the intrinsic properties of bodies when their external circumstances are varying. But however it arises, congruence is in essence the correlation of two regions of space, point by point, so that all homologous distances and all homologous angles are equal. It is to be noticed that the definition of the equality of lengths and angles is their congruence, and all tests of equality, such as the use of the yard measure, are merely devices for making immediate judgments of congruence easy. I make these remarks to suggest that apart from the reasoning connected with it, congruence, both as an example of a larger and very far-reaching idea and also for its own sake, is well worthy of attentive consideration. The propositions concerning it elucidate the elementary properties of the triangle, the parallelogram, and the circle, and of the relations of two planes to each other. It is very desirable to restrict the proved propositions of this part within the narrowest bounds, partly by assuming redundant axiomatic propositions, and partly by introducing only those propositions of absolutely fundamental importance.

The second stage is the study of similarity. This can be reduced to three or four fundamental propositions. Similarity is an enlargement of the idea of congruence, and, like that idea, is another example of a one-to-one correlation of points of spaces. Any extension of study of this subject might well be in the direction of the investigation of one or two simple properties of similar and similarly situated rectilinear figures. The whole subject receives its immediate applications in plans and maps. It is important, however, to remember that trigonometry is really the method by which the main theorems are made available for use.

The third stage is the study of the elements of trigonometry. This is the study of the periodicity introduced by rotation and of properties preserved in a correlation of similar figures. Here for the first time we introduce a slight use of the algebraic analysis founded on the study of number and quantity. The importance of the periodic character of the functions requires full illustration. The simplest properties of the functions are the only ones required for the solution of triangles, and the consequent applications to surveying. The wealth of formulæ, often important in themselves, but entirely useless for this type of study, which crowd our books should be rigorously excluded, except so far as they are capable of being proved by the pupils as direct examples of the bookwork.

This question of the exclusion of formulæ is best illustrated by considering this example of Trigonometry, though of course I may well have hit on an unfortunate case in which my judgment is at fault.   A great part of the educational advantage of the subject can be obtained by confining study to Trigonometry of one angle and by exclusion of the addition formulæ for the sine and cosine of the sum of two angles. The functions can be graphed, and the solution of triangles effected.   Thus the aspects of the science as (1) embodying analytically the immediate results of some of the theorems deduced from congruence and similarity, (2) as a solution of the main problem of surveying, (3) as a study of the fundamental functions required to express periodicity and wave motion, will all be impressed on the pupils' minds both by bookwork and example.

If it be desired to extend this course, the addition formulæ should be added.   But great care should be taken to exclude specialising the pupils in the wealth of formulæ which comes in their train.   By " exclude " is meant that the pupils should not have spent time or energy in acquiring any facility in their deduction. The teacher may find it interesting to work a few such examples before a class.   But such results are not among those which learners need retain. Also, I would exclude the whole subject of circumscribed and inscribed circles both from Trigonometry and from the previous geometrical courses. It is all very pretty, but I do not understand what its function is in an elementary non-professional curriculum.

Accordingly, the actual bookwork of the subject is reduced to very manageable proportions. I was told the other day of an American college where the students are expected to know by heart ninety formulæ or results in Trigonometry alone. We are not quite so bad as that. In fact, in Trigonometry we have nearly approached the ideal here sketched out as far as our elementary courses are concerned.

The fourth stage introduces Analytical Geometry. The study of graphs in algebra has already employed the fundamental notions, and all that is now required is a rigorously pruned course on the straight line, the circle, and the three types of conic sections, defined by the forms of their equations. At this point there are two remarks to be made. It is often desirable to give our pupils mathematical information which we do not prove. For example, in co-ordinate geometry, the reduction of the general equation of the second degree is probably beyond the capacities of most of the type of students whom we are considering. But that need not prevent us from explaining the fundamental position of conics, as exhausting the possible types of such curves.

The second remark is to advocate the entire sweeping away of geometrical conics as a separate subject. Naturally, on suitable occasions the analysis of analytical geometry will be lightened by the use of direct deduction from some simple figure. But geometrical conics, as developed from the definition of a conic section by the focus and directrix property, suffers from glaring defects. It is hopelessly recondite. The fundamental definition of a conic, $SP = e . PM$, usual in this subject at this stage, is thoroughly bad. It is very recondite, and has no obvious importance. Why should such curves be studied at all, any more than those defined by an indefinite number of other formulæ? But when we have commenced the study of the Cartesian methods, the equations of the first and second degrees are naturally the first things to think about.

In this ideal course of Geometry, the fifth stage is occupied with the elements of Projective Geometry. The general ideas of cross ratio and of projection are here fundamental. Projection is yet a more general instance of that one-to-one correlation which we have already considered under congruence and similarity. Here again we must avoid the danger of being led into a bewildering wealth of detail.

The intellectual idea which projective geometry
is to illustrate is the importance in reasoning of
the correlation of all cases which can be proved
to possess in common certain identical properties.
The preservation of the projective properties in
projection is the one important educational idea of
the subject. Cross ratio only enters as the fundamental metrical property which is preserved.
The few propositions considered are selected to
illustrate the two allied processes which are
made possible by this procedure. One is proof
by simplification. Here the simplification is
psychological and not logical—for the general
case is logically the simplest. What is meant
is : Proof by considering the case which is in
fact the most familiar to us, or the easiest to
think about. The other procedure is the deduction of particular cases from known general truths,
as soon as we have a means of discovering such
cases or a criterion for testing them.

The projective definition of conic sections and
the identity of the results obtained with the
curves derived from the general equation of the
second degree are capable of simple exposition,
but lie on the border-line of the subject. It is
the sort of topic on which information can be
given, and the proofs suppressed.

The course of geometry as here conceived in
its complete ideal—and ideals can never be
realised—is not a long one. The actual amount

of mathematical deduction at each stage in the form of bookwork is very slight. But much more explanation would be given, the importance of each proposition being illustrated by examples, either worked out or for students to work, so selected as to indicate the fields of thought to which it applies. By such a course the student would gain an analysis of the leading properties of space, and of the chief methods by which they are investigated.

The study of the elements of mathematics, conceived in this spirit, would constitute a training in logical method together with an acquisition of the precise ideas which lie at the base of the scientific and philosophical investigations of the universe. Would it be easy to continue the excellent reforms in mathematical instruction which this generation has already achieved, so as to include in the curriculum this wider and more philosophic spirit? Frankly, I think that this result would be very hard to achieve as the result of single individual efforts. For reasons which I have already briefly indicated, all reforms in education are very difficult to effect. But the continued pressure of combined effort, provided that the ideal is really present in the minds of the mass of teachers, can do much, and effects in the end surprising modification. Gradually the requisite books get written, still more gradually the examinations are reformed so as to give weight to the less technical aspects of the subject, and then all recent experience has shown that the majority of teachers are only too ready to welcome any practicable means of rescuing the subject from the reproach of being a mechanical discipline.

CHAPTER V

THE PRINCIPLES OF MATHEMATICS IN RELATION TO ELEMENTARY TEACHING

(International Congress of Mathematicians, Cambridge, August, 1912)

WE are concerned not with the advanced teaching of a few specialist mathematical students, but with the mathematical education of the majority of boys in our secondary schools. Again these boys must be divided into two sections: one section consists of those who desire to restrict their mathematical education; the other section is made up of those who will require some mathematical training for their subsequent professional careers, either in the form of definite mathematical results or in the form of mathematically trained minds.

I shall call the latter of these two sections the mathematical section, and the former the non-mathematical section. But I must repeat that by the mathematical section is meant that large number of boys who desire to learn more than the minimum amount of mathematics. Furthermore, most of my remarks about these sections of boys apply also to elementary classes of our University students.

The subject of this paper is the investigation of the place which should be occupied by modern investigations respecting mathematical principles in the education of both of these sections of school-boys.

To find a foothold from which to start the inquiry, let us ask why the non-mathematical section should be taught any mathematics at all beyond the barest elements of arithmetic. What are the qualities of mind which a mathematical training is designed to produce when it is employed as an element in a liberal education ?

My answer, which applies equally to both sections of students, is that there are two allied forms of mental discipline which should be acquired by a well-designed mathematical course. These two forms though closely allied are perfectly distinct.

The first form of discipline is not in its essence logical at all. It is the power of clearly grasping abstract ideas, and of relating them to particular circumstances. In other words, the first use of mathematics is to strengthen the power of abstract thought. I repeat that in its essence this has nothing to do with logic, though as a matter of fact a logical discipline is the best method of producing the desired effect. It is not the philo-sophical theory of abstract ideas which is to be acquired, but the habit and the power of using them. There is one and only way of acquiring the habit and the power of using anything, that is by the simple common-place method of habitually using it. There is no other short cut. If in education we desire to produce a certain conformation of mind, we must day by day, and year by year, accustom the students' minds to grow into the desired structural shape. Thus to teach the power of grasping abstract ideas and the habit of using them, we must select a group of such ideas, which are important and are also easy to think about because they are clear and definite.

The fundamental mathematical truths concerning geometry, ratio, quantity, and number, satisfy these conditions as do no others. Hence, the fundamental universal position held by mathematics as an element of a liberal education.

But what are the fundamental mathematical truths concerning geometry, quantity and number?

At this point we come to the great question of the relation between the modern science of the principles of mathematics and a mathematical education.

My answer to the question as to these fundamental mathematical truths is, that in any absolute sense there are none. There is no unique small body of independent primitive unproved propositions which are the necessary starting points of all mathematical reasoning on these subjects. In mathematical reasoning the only absolute necessary pre-suppositions are those which make logical deduction possible. Between these absolute logical truths and so-called fundamental truths concerning geometry, quantity and number, there is a whole new world of mathematical subjects concerning the logic of propositions, of classes, and of relations.

But this subject is too abstract to form an elementary training ground in the difficult art of abstract thought.

It is for this reason that we have to make a compromise and start from such obvious general ideas as naturally occur to all men when they perceive objects with their senses.

In geometry, the ideas elaborated by the Greeks and presented by Euclid are, roughly speaking, those adapted for our purpose, namely, ideas of volumes, surfaces, lines, of straightness and of curvature, of intersection and of congruence, of greater and less, of similarity, shape, and scale. In fact, we use in education those general ideas of spatial properties which must be habitually present in the mind of any one who is to observe the world of phenomena with understanding.

Thus we come back to Plato's opinion that for a liberal education, geometry, as he knew it, is the queen of sciences.

In addition' to geometry, there remain the ideas of quantity, ratio, and of number. This in practice means, elementary algebra. Here the prominent ideas are those of " any number," in other words, the use of the familiar x, y, z, and of the dependence of variables on each other, or otherwise, the idea of functionality. All this is to be gradually acquired by the continual use of the very simplest functions which we can devise: of linear functions, graphically represented by straight lines; of quadratic functions, graphically represented by parabolas; and of those simple implicit functions, graphically represented by conic sections. Thence, with good fortune and a willing class, we can advance to the ideas of rates of increase, still confining ourselves to the simplest possible cases.

I wish here emphatically to remind you that both in geometry and in algebra a clear grasp of these general ideas is not what the pupil starts from, it is the goal at which he is to arrive. The method of progression is continual practice in the consideration of the simplest particular cases, and the goal is not philosophical analysis but the power of use.

But how is he to practise himself in their use? He cannot simply sit down and think of the relation $y = x + 1$, he must employ it in some simple obvious way.

This brings us to the second power of mind

which is to be produced by a mathematical training, namely, the power of logical reasoning. Here
again, it is not the knowledge of the philosophy
of logic which it is essential to teach, but the habit
of thinking logically. By logic, I mean deductive
logic.

Deductive logic is the science of certain relations, such as implication, etc., between general
ideas. When logic begins, definite particular
individual things have been banished. I cannot
relate logically this thing to that thing, for
example this pen to that pen, except by the indirect way of relating some general idea which
applies to this pen to some general idea which
applies to that pen. And the individualities of
the two pens are quite irrelevant to the logical
process. This process is entirely concerned with
the two general ideas. Thus the practice of logic
is a certain way of employing the mind in the
consideration of such ideas; and an elementary
mathematical training is in fact nothing else but
the logical use of the general ideas respecting
geometry and algebra which we have enumerated
above. It has therefore, as I started this paper
by stating, a double advantage. It makes the
mind capable of abstract thought, and it achieves
this object by training the mind in the most
important kind of abstract thought, namely,
deductive logic.

I may remind you that other choices of a type

H

of abstract thought might be made. We might train the children to contemplate directly the beauty of abstract moral ideas, in the hope of making them religious mystics. The general practice of education has· decided in favour of logic, as exemplified in elementary mathematics.

We have now to answer the further question, what is the rôle of logical precision in the teaching of mathematics ? Our general answer to the implied question is obvious : logical precision is one of the two objects of the teaching of mathematics, and it is the only weapon by which the teaching of mathematics can achieve its other object. To teach mathematics is to teach logical precision. A mathematical teacher who has not taught that has taught nothing.

But having stated this thesis in this unqualified way, its meaning must be carefully explained; for otherwise its real bearing on the problem will be entirely misunderstood.

Logical precision is the faculty to be acquired. It is the quality of mind which it is the object of the teaching to impart. Thus the habit of reading great literature is the goal at which a literary education aims. But we do not expect a child to start its first lesson by reading for itself Shakespeare. We recognise that reading is impossible till the pupil has learnt its alphabet and can spell, and then we start it with books of one syllable.

In the same way, a mathematical education should grow in logical precision. It is folly to expect the same careful logical analysis at the commencement of the training as would be appropriate at the end. It is an entire misconception of my thesis to construe it as meaning that a mathematical training should assume in the pupil a power of concentrated logical thought. My thesis is in fact the exact opposite, namely, that this power cannot be assumed, and has got to be acquired, and that a mathematical training is nothing else than the process of acquiring it. My whole groundwork of assumption is that this power does not initially exist in a fully developed state. Of course like every other power which is acquired, it must be developed gradually.

The various stages of development must be guided by the judgment and the genius of the teacher. But what is essential is, that the teacher should keep clearly in his mind that it is just this power of logical precise reasoning which is the whole object of his efforts. If his pupils have in any measure gained this, they have gained all.

We have not yet, however, fully considered this part of our subject. Logical precision is the full realisation of the steps of the argument. But what are the steps of the argument? The full statement of all the steps is far too elaborate and difficult an operation to be introduced into the mathematical reasoning of an educational

curriculum.   Such a statement involves the introduction of abstract logical ideas which are very
difficult to grasp, because there is so rarely any
need to make them explicit in ordinary thought.
They are therefore not a fit subject-ground for
an elementary education.

I do not think that it is possible to draw any
theoretical line between those logical steps which
form a theoretically full logical investigation,
and those which are full enough for most practical purposes, including that of education.   The
question is one of psychology, to be solved by a
process of experiment.   The object to be attained
is to gain that amount of logical alertness which
will enable its possessors to detect fallacy and to
know the types of sound logical deduction.   The
objects of going further are partly philosophical,
and also partly to lay bare abstract ideas whose
investigation is in itself important.   But both
these objects are foreign to education.

My opinion is, that, on the whole, the type of
logical precision handed down to us by the Greek
mathematicians is, roughly speaking, what we
want.   In geometry, this means the sort of precision which we find in Euclid.   I do not mean
that we should use his famous *Elements* as a
text-book, nor that here and there a certain com-
pression in his mode of exposition is not advisable.
All this is mere detail.   What I do mean is,
that the sort of logical transition which he made

explicit, we should make explicit, and that the sort of transition which he omits, we should omit.

I doubt, however, whether it is desirable to plunge the student into the full rigour of euclidean geometry without some mitigation. It is for this reason that the modern habit, at least in England, of laying great stress in the initial stages on training the pupil in simple constructions from numerical data is to be praised. It means that after a slight amount of reasoning on the euclidean basis of accuracy, the mind of the learner is relieved by doing the things in various special cases, and noting by rough measurements that the desired results are actually attained. It is important, however, that the measurements be not mistaken for the proofs. Their object is to make the beginner apprehend what the abstract ideas really mean.

Again in algebra, the notation and the practical use of the symbols should be acquired in the simplest cases, and the more theoretical treatment of the symbolism reserved to a suitable later stage. My rule would be initially to learn the meaning of the ideas by a crude practice in simple ways, and to refine the logical procedure in preparation for an advance to greater generality. In fact the thesis of my paper can be put in another way thus, the object of a mathematical education is, to acquire the powers of analysis, of generalisation, and of reasoning. The two processes of analysis and generalisation were in my previous statement put together as the power of grasping abstract ideas.

But in order to analyse and to generalise, we must commence with the crude material of ideas which are to be analysed and generalised. Accordingly it is a positive error in education to start with the ultimate products of this process, namely the ideas in their refined analysed and generalised forms. We are thereby skipping an important part of the training, which is to take the ideas as they actually exist in the child's mind, and to exercise the child in the difficult art of civilising them and clothing them.

The schoolmaster is in fact a missionary, the savages are the ideas in the child's mind; and the missionary shirks his main task if he refuse to risk his body among the cannibals.

At this point I should like to turn your attention to those pupils forming the mathematical section. There is an idea, widely prevalent, that it is possible to teach mathematics of a relatively advanced type—such as differential calculus, for instance—in a way useful to physicists and engineers without any attention to its logic or its theory.

This seems to me to be a profound mistake. It implies that a merely mechanical knowledge without understanding of ways of arriving at mathematical results is useful in applied science. It is of no use whatever. The results themselves can all be found stated in the appropriate pocket books and in other elementary works of reference. No one when applying a result need bother himself as to why it is true. He accepts it and applies it. What is of supreme importance in physics and in engineering is a mathematically trained mind, and such a mind can only be acquired by a proper mathematical discipline.

I fully admit that the proper way to start such a subject as the differential calculus is to plunge quickly into the use of the notation in a few absurdly simple cases, with a crude explanation of the idea of rates of increase. The notation as thus known can then be used by the lecturers in the Physical and Engineering Laboratories. But the mathematical training of the applied scientists consists in making these ideas precise and the proofs accurate.

I hope that the thesis of this paper respecting the position of logical precision in the teaching of mathematics has been rendered plain. The habit of logical precision with its necessary concentration of thought upon abstract ideas is not wholly possible in the initial stages of learning. It is the ideal at which the teacher should aim. Also logical precision, in the sense of logical explicitness, is not an absolute thing : it is an affair of more or less. Accordingly the quantity of explicitness to be introduced at each stage of progress must depend upon the practical judgment of the teacher. Lastly, in a sense, the instructed mind is less explicit; for it travels more quickly over a well-remembered path, and may save the trouble of putting into words trains of thought which are very obvious to it. But on the other hand it atones for this rapidity by a concentration on every subtle point where a fallacy can lurk. The habit of logical precision is the instinct for the subtle difficulty.

CHAPTER VI

THE ORGANISATION OF THOUGHT

(*Presidential Address to Section A, British Association, Newcastle, 1916*)

THE subject of this address is the organisation of thought, a topic evidently capable of many diverse modes of treatment. I intend more particularly to give some account of that department of logical science with which some of my own studies have been connected. But I am anxious, if I can succeed in so doing, to handle this account so as to exhibit the relation with certain considerations which underlie general scientific activities.

It is no accident that an age of science has developed into an age of organisation. Organised thought is the basis of organised action. Organisation is the adjustment of diverse elements so that their mutual relations may exhibit some predetermined quality. An epic poem is a triumph of organisation, that is to say, it is a triumph in the unlikely event of its being a good epic poem. It is the successful organisation of multitudinous sounds of words, associations of words, pictorial memories of diverse events and feelings ordinarily occurring in life, combined with a special narrative of great events : the whole so disposed as to excite emotions which, as defined by Milton, are simple, sensuous, and passionate. The number of successful epic poems is commensurate, or rather, is inversely commensurate, with the obvious difficulty of the task of organisation.

Science is the organisation of thought. But the example of the epic poem warns us that science is not any organisation of thought. It is an organisation of a certain definite type which we will endeavour to determine.

Science is a river with two sources, the practical source and the theoretical source. The practical source is the desire to direct our actions to achieve predetermined ends. For example, the British nation, fighting for justice, turns to science, which teaches it the importance of compounds of nitrogen. The theoretical source is the desire to understand. Now I am going to emphasise the importance of theory in science. But to avoid misconception I most emphatically state that I do not consider one source as in any sense nobler than the other, or intrinsically more interesting. I cannot see why it is nobler to strive to understand than to busy oneself with the right ordering of one's actions. Both have their bad sides; there are evil ends directing actions, and there are ignoble curiosities of the understanding.

The importance, even in practice, of the theoretical side of science arises from the fact that action must be immediate, and takes place under circumstances which are excessively complicated. If we wait for the necessities of action before we commence to arrange our ideas, in peace we shall have lost our trade, and in war we shall have lost the battle. Success in practice depends on theorists who, led by other motives of exploration, have been there before, and by some good chance have hit upon the relevant ideas. By a theorist I do not mean a man who is up in the clouds, but a man whose motive for thought is the desire to formulate correctly the rules according to which events occur. A successful theorist should be excessively interested in immediate events, otherwise he is not at all likely to formulate correctly anything about them. Of course, both sources of science exist in all men.

Now, what is this thought organisation which we call science? The first aspect of modern science which struck thoughtful observers was its inductive character. The nature of induction, its importance, and the rules of inductive logic have been considered by a long series of thinkers, especially English thinkers: Bacon, Herschel, J. S. Mill, Venn, Jevons, and others. I am not going to plunge into an analysis of the

process of induction. Induction is the machinery
and not the product, and it is the product which
I want to consider. When we understand the
product we shall be in a stronger position to
improve the machinery.

First, there is one point which it is necessary
to emphasise. There is a tendency in analysing
scientific processes to assume a given assemblage
of concepts applying to nature, and to imagine
that the discovery of laws of nature consists in
selecting by means of inductive logic some one
out of a definite set of possible alternative relations which may hold between the things in
nature answering to these obvious concepts. In
a sense this assumption is fairly correct, especially
in regard to the earlier stages of science. Mankind found itself in possession of certain concepts
respecting nature—for example, the concept of
fairly permanent material bodies—and proceeded
to determine laws which related the corresponding percepts in nature. But the formulation of
laws changed the concepts, sometimes gently by
an added precision, sometimes violently. At first
this process was not much noticed, or at least
was felt to be a process curbed within narrow
bounds, not touching fundamental ideas. At the
stage where we now are, the formulation of
the concepts can be seen to be as important as
the formulation of the empirical laws connecting the events in the universe as thus conceived

by us. For example, the concepts of life, of he-
redity, of a material body, of a molecule, of
an atom, of an electron, of energy, of space, of
time, of quantity, and of number. I am not
dogmatising about the best way of getting such
ideas straight. Certainly it will only be done by
those who have devoted themselves to a special
study of the facts in question. Success is never
absolute, and progress in the right direction is
the result of a slow, gradual process of continual
comparison of ideas with facts. The criterion
of success is that we should be able to formulate
empirical laws, that is, statements of relations,
connecting the various parts of the universe as
thus conceived, laws with the property that we
can interpret the actual events of our lives as
being our fragmentary knowledge of this conceived interrelated whole.

But, for the purpose of science, what is the
actual world ? Has science to wait for the ter-
mination of the metaphysical debate till it can
determine its own subject-matter ? I suggest
that science has a much more homely starting-
ground. Its task is the discovery of the relations
which exist within that flux of perceptions, sensa-
tions, and emotions which forms our experience
of life. The panorama yielded by sight, sound,
taste, smell, touch, and by more inchoate sensible
feelings, is the sole field of activity. It is in this
way that science is the thought organisation of

experience. The most obvious aspect of this field of actual experience is its disorderly character. It is for each person a *continuum,* fragmentary, and with elements not clearly differentiated. The comparison of the sensible experiences of diverse people brings its own difficulties. I insist on the radically untidy, ill-adjusted character of the fields of actual experience from which science starts. To grasp this fundamental truth is the first step in wisdom, when constructing a philosophy of science. This fact is concealed by the influence of language, moulded by science, which foists on us exact concepts as though they represented the immediate deliverances of experience. The result is, that we imagine that we have immediate experience of a world of perfectly defined objects implicated in perfectly defined events which, as known to us by the direct deliverance of our senses, happen at exact instants of time, in a space formed by exact points, without parts and without magnitude : the neat, trim, tidy, exact world which is the goal of scientific thought.

My contention is, that this world is a world of ideas, and that its internal relations are relations between abstract concepts, and that the elucidation of the precise connection between this world and the feelings of actual experience is the fundamental question of scientific philosophy. The question which I am inviting you to con-

sider is this : How does exact thought apply to
the fragmentary, vague *continua* of experience ?
I am not saying that it does not apply : quite the
contrary. But I want to know how it applies.
The solution I am asking for is not a phrase,
however brilliant, but a solid branch of science,
constructed with slow patience, showing in detail
how the correspondence is effected.

The first great steps in the organisation of
thought were due exclusively to the practical
source of scientific activity, without any admix-
ture of theoretical impulse. Their slow accomplishment was the cause and also the effect of
the gradual evolution of moderately rational
beings. I mean the formation of the concepts
of definite material objects, of the determinate
lapse of time, of simultaneity, of recurrence, of
definite relative position, and of analogous fundamental ideas, according to which the flux of our
experience is mentally arranged for handy reference : in fact, the whole apparatus of commonsense thought. Consider in your mind some
definite chair. The concept of that chair is simply
the concept of all the interrelated experiences
connected with that chair—namely, of the experience of the folk who made it, of the folk who
sold it, of the folk who have seen it or used it,
of the man who is now experiencing a comfort-
able sense of support, combined with our expectations of an analogous future, terminated finally

by a different set of experiences when the chair
collapses and becomes firewood. The formation of that type of concept was a tremendous
job, and zoologists and geologists tell us that it
took many tens of millions of years. I can well
believe it.

I now emphasise two points. In the first
place, science is rooted in what I have just called
the whole apparatus of commonsense thought.
That is the *datum* from which it starts, and to
which it must recur. We may speculate, if it
amuses us, of other beings in other planets who
have arranged analogous experiences according to an ,entirely different conceptual code—
namely, who have directed their chief attention
to different relations between their various experiences. But the task is too complex, too
gigantic, to be revised in its main outlines. You
may polish up commonsense, you may contradict
it in detail, you may surprise it. But ultimately
your whole task is to satisfy it.

In the second place, neither commonsense nor
science can proceed with their task of thought
organisation without departing in some respect
from the strict consideration of what is actual in
experience. Think again of the chair. Among
the experiences upon which its concept is based,
I included our expectations of its future history.
I should have gone further and included our
imagination of all the possible experiences which

in ordinary language we should call perceptions of the chair which might have occurred. This is a difficult question, and I do not see my way through it. But, at present, in the construction of a theory of space and of time there seem insuperable difficulties if we refuse to admit ideal experiences.

This imaginative perception of experiences, which, if they occurred, would be coherent with our actual experiences, seems fundamental in our lives. It is neither wholly arbitrary, nor yet fully determined. It is a vague background which is only made in part definite by isolated activities of thought. Consider, for example, our thoughts of the unseen flora of Brazil.

Ideal experiences are closely connected with our imaginative reproduction of the actual experiences of other people, and also with our almost inevitable conception of ourselves as receiving our impressions from an external complex reality beyond ourselves. It may be that an adequate analysis of every source and every type of experience yields demonstrative proof of such a reality and of its nature. Indeed, it is hardly to be doubted that this is the case. The precise elucidation of this question is the problem of metaphysics. One of the points which I am urging in this address is, that the basis of science does not depend on the assumption of any of the conclusions of metaphysics; but that both

I

science and metaphysics start from the same given groundwork of immediate experience, and in the main proceed in opposite directions on their diverse tasks.

For example, metaphysics inquires how our perceptions of the chair relate us to some true reality. Science gathers up these perceptions into a determinate class, adds to them ideal perceptions of analogous sort, which under assignable circumstances would be obtained, and this single concept of that set of perceptions is all that science needs; unless indeed you prefer that thought find its origin in some legend of those great twin brethren, the Cock and Bull.

My immediate problem is to inquire into the nature of the texture of science. Science is essentially logical. The nexus between its concepts is a logical nexus, and the grounds for its detailed assertions are logical grounds. King James said, "No bishops, no king." With greater confidence we can say, "No logic, no science." The reason for the instinctive dislike which most men of science feel towards the recognition of this truth is, I think, the barren failure of logical theory during the past three or four centuries. We may trace this failure back to the worship of authority, which in some respects increased in the learned world at the time of the Renaissance. Mankind then changed its authority, and this fact temporally acted as an emancipation. But the main fact, and we can find complaints [1] of it at the very commencement of the modern movement, was the establishment of a reverential attitude towards any statement made by a classical author. Scholars became commentators on truths too fragile to bear translation. A science which hesitates to forget its founders is lost. To this hesitation I ascribe the barrenness of logic. Another reason for distrust of logical theory and of mathematics is the belief that deductive reasoning can give you nothing new. Your conclusions are contained in your premises, which by hypothesis are known to you.

In the first place this last condemnation of logic neglects the fragmentary, disconnected character of human knowledge. To know one premise on Monday, and another premise on Tuesday, is useless to you on Wednesday. Science is a permanent record of premises, deductions, and conclusions, verified all along the line by its correspondence with facts. Secondly, it is untrue that when we know the premises we also know the conclusions. In arithmetic, for examample, mankind are not calculating boys. Any theory which proves that they are conversant with the consequences of their assumptions must be wrong. We can imagine beings who possess such insight. But we are not such creatures.

[1] *E. g.* in 1551 by Italian schoolmen; cf. Sarpi's *History of the Council of Trent,* under that date.

Both these answers are, I think, true and relevant. But they are not satisfactory. They are too much in the nature of bludgeons, too external. We want something more explanatory of the very real difficulty which the question suggests. In fact, the true answer is embedded in the discussion of our main problem of the relation of logic to natural science.

It will be necessary to sketch in broad outline some relevant features of modern logic. In doing so I shall try to avoid the profound general discussions and the minute technical classifications which occupy the main part of traditional logic. It is characteristic of a science in its earlier stages —and logic has become fossilised in such a stage —to be both ambitiously profound in its aims and trivial in its handling of details.

We can discern four departments of logical theory. By an analogy which is not so very remote I will call these departments or sections the arithmetic section, the algebraic section, the section of general-function theory, the analytical section. I do not mean that arithmetic arises in the first section, algebra in the second section, and so on; but the names are suggestive of certain qualities of thought in each section which are reminiscent of analogous qualities in arithmetic, in algebra, in the general theory of a mathematical function, and in the mathematical analysis of the properties of particular functions.

The first section—namely, the arithmetic stage —deals with the relations of definite propositions to each other, just as arithmetic deals with definite numbers. Consider any definite proposition; call it " p." We conceive that there is always another proposition which is the direct contradictory to " p "; call it " not-p." When we have got two propositions, p and q, we can form derivative propositions from them, and from their contradictories. We can say, " At last one of p or q is true, and perhaps both." Let us call this proposition " p or q." I may mention as an aside that one of the greatest living philosophers has stated that this use of the word " or "— namely, " p or q " in the sense that either or both may be true—makes him despair of exact expression. We must brave his wrath, which is unintelligible to me.

We have thus got hold of four new propositions, namely, " p or q," and " not-p or q," and " p or not-q," and " not-p or not-q." Call these the set of disjunctive derivatives. There are, so far, in all eight propositions, p, not-p, q, not-q, and the four disjunctive derivatives. Any pair of these eight propositions can be taken, and substituted for p and q in the foregoing treatment. Thus each pair yields eight propositions, some of which may have been obtained before. By proceeding in this way we arrive at an unending set of propositions of growing complexity, ultimately derived from the two original propositions p or q. Of course, only a few are important. Similarly we can start from three propositions, p, q, r, or from four propositions, p, q, r, s, and so on. Any one of the propositions of these aggregates may be true or false. It has no other alternative. Whichever it is, true or false, call it the " truth-value " of the proposition.

The first section of logical inquiry is to settle what we know of the truth-values of these propositions, when we know the truth-values of some of them. The inquiry, so far as it is worth while carrying it, is not very abstruse, and the best way of expressing its results is a detail which I will not now consider. This inquiry forms the arithmetic stage.

The next section of logic is the algebraic stage. Now, the difference between arithmetic and algebra is, that in arithmetic definite numbers are considered, and in algebra symbols—namely, letters—are introduced which stand for any numbers. The idea of a number is also enlarged. These letters, standing for any numbers, are called sometimes variables and sometimes parameters. Their essential characteristic is that they are undetermined, unless, indeed, the algebraic conditions which they satisfy implicitly determine them. Then they are sometimes called unknowns. An algebraic formula with letters is a blank form. It becomes a determinate arithmetic

statement when definite numbers are substituted
for the letters.   The importance of algebra is a
tribute to the study of form.   Consider now the
following proposition—

The specific heat of mercury is 0·033.

This is a definite proposition which, with certain
limitations, is true.   But the truth-value of the
proposition does not immediately concern us.
Instead of mercury put a mere letter which is the
name of some undetermined thing : we get—

The specific heat of x is 0·033.

This is not a proposition; it has been called by
Russell a propositional function.   It is the logical
analogy of an algebraic expression.   Let us write
$f(x)$ for any propositional function.

We could also generalise still further, and say,

The specific heat of x is y.

We thus get another propositional function,
$F(x, y)$, of two arguments x and y, and so on
for any number of arguments.

Now, consider $f(x)$.   There is the range of
values of x, for which $f(x)$ is a proposition, true
or false.   For values of x outside this range, $f(x)$
is not a proposition at all, and is neither true nor
false.   It may have vague suggestions for us,
but it has no unit meaning of definite assertion.
For example,

The specific heat of water is 0·033

is a proposition which is false; and—

The specific heat of virtue is 0·033

is, I should imagine, not a proposition at all; so that it is neither true nor false, though its component parts raise various associations in our minds. This range of values, for which $f(x)$ has sense, is called the " type " of the argument x.

But there is also a range of values of x for which $f(x)$ is a true proposition. This is the class of those values of the argument which *satisfy* $f(x)$. This class may have no members, or, in the other extreme, the class may be the whole type of the arguments.

We thus conceive two general propositions respecting the indefinite number of propositions which share in the same logical form, that is, which are values of the same propositional function. One of these propositions is,

$f(x)$ yields a true proposition for each value
of x of the proper type;

the other proposition is,

There is a value of x for which $f(x)$ is true.

Given two, or more, propositional functions $f(x)$ and $\phi(x)$ with the same argument x, we form derivative propositional functions, namely,

$f(x)$ or $\phi(x)$, $f(x)$ or not-$\phi(x)$,

and so on with the contradictories, obtaining, as

in the arithmetical stage, an unending aggregate of propositional functions. Also each propositional function yields two general propositions. The theory of the interconnection between the truth-values of the general propositions arising from any such aggregate of propositional functions forms a simple and elegant chapter of mathematical logic.

In this algebraic section of logic the theory of types crops up, as we have already noted. It cannot be neglected without the introduction of error. Its theory has to be settled at least by some safe hypothesis, even if it does not go to the philosophic basis of the question. This part of the subject is obscure and difficult, and has not been finally elucidated, though Russell's brilliant work has opened out the subject.

The final impulse to modern logic comes from the independent discovery of the importance of the logic variable by Frege and Peano. Frege went further than Peano, but by an unfortunate symbolism rendered his work so obscure that no one fully recognised his meaning who had not found it out for himself. But the movement has a large history reaching back to Leibniz and even to Aristotle. Among English contributors are De Morgan, Boole, and Sir Alfred Kempe; their work is of the first rank.

The third logical section is the stage of general-function theory. In logical language, we perform in this stage the transition from intension to extension, and investigate the theory of denotation. Take the propositional function $f(x)$. There is the class, or range of values for x, whose members satisfy $f(x)$. But the same range may be the class whose members satisfy another propositional function $\phi(x)$. It is necessary to investigate how to indicate the class by a way which is indifferent as between the various propositional functions which are satisfied by any member of it, and of it only. What has to be done is to analyse the nature of propositions about a class—namely, those propositions whose truth-values depend on the class itself and not on the particular meaning by which the class is indicated.

Furthermore, there are propositions about alleged individuals indicated by descriptive phrases : for example, propositions about " the present King of England," who does exist, and " the present Emperor of Brazil," who does not exist. More complicated, but analogous, questions involving propositional functions of two variables involve the notion of " correlation," just as functions of one argument involve classes. Similarly functions of three arguments yield three-cornered correlations, and so on. This logical section is one which Russell has made peculiarly his own by work which must always remain fundamental. I have called this the section of functional theory, because its ideas are essential to the construction of logical denoting functions which include as a special case ordinary mathematical functions, such as sine, logarithm, etc. In each of these three stages it will be necessary gradually to introduce an appropriate symbolism, if we are to pass on to the fourth stage.

The fourth logical section, the analytic stage, is concerned with the investigation of the properties of special logical constructions, that is, of classes and correlations of special sorts. The whole of mathematics is included here. So the section is a large one. In fact, it is mathematics, neither more nor less, but it includes an analysis of mathematical ideas not hitherto included in the scope of that science, nor, indeed, contemplated at all. The essence of this stage is construction. It is by means of suitable constructions that the great framework of applied mathematics, comprising the theories of number, quantity, time, and space, is elaborated.

It is impossible, even in brief outline, to explain how mathematics is developed from the concepts of class and correlation, including many-cornered correlations, which are established in the third section. I can only allude to the headings of the process, which is fully developed in the work, *Principia Mathematica,* by Mr. Russell and myself. There are in this process of development seven special sorts of correlations which are of peculiar interest. The first sort comprises one-to-many, many-to-one, and one-to-one correlations. The second sort comprises serial relations, that is, correlations by which the members of some field are arranged in serial order, so that, in the sense defined by the relation, any member of the field is either before or after any other member. The third class comprises inductive relations, that is, correlations on which the theory of mathematical induction depends. The fourth class comprises selective relations, which are required for the general theory of arithmetic operations, and elsewhere. It is in connection with such relations that the famous multiplicative axiom arises for consideration. The fifth class comprises vector relations, from which the theory of quantity arises. The sixth class comprises ratio relations, which interconnect number and quantity. The seventh class comprises three-cornered and four-cornered relations which occur in geometry.

A bare enumeration of technical names, such as the above, is not very illuminating, though it may help to a comprehension of the demarcations of the subject. Please remember that the names are technical names, meant, no doubt, to be suggestive, but used in strictly defined senses. We have suffered much from critics who consider it sufficient to criticise our procedure on the slender basis of a knowledge of the dictionary meanings of such terms. For example, a one-to-one correlation depends on the notion of a class with only one member, and this notion is defined without appeal to the concept of the number one. The notion of diversity is all that is wanted. Thus the class a has only one member, if (1) the class of values of x which satisfies the propositional function,

x is not a member of a,

is not the whole type of relevant values of x, and if (2) the propositional function,

x and y are members of a, and x is diverse from y

is false, whatever be the values of x and y in the relevant type.

Analogous procedures are obviously possible for higher finite cardinal members. Thus, step by step, the whole cycle of current mathematical ideas is capable of logical definition. The process is detailed and laborious, and, like all science, knows nothing of a royal road of airy phrases. The essence of the process is, first, to construct the notion in terms of the forms of propositions, that is, in terms of the relevant propositional functions, and secondly, to prove the fundamental truths which hold about the notion by reference to the results obtained in the algebraic section of logic.

It will be seen that in this process the whole apparatus of special indefinable mathematical concepts, and special *a priori* mathematical premises, respecting number, quantity, and space, has vanished. Mathematics is merely an apparatus for analysing the deductions which can be drawn from any particular premises, supplied by common sense, or by more refined scientific observation, so far as these deductions depend on the forms of the propositions. Propositions of certain forms are continually occurring in thought. Our existing mathematics is the analysis of deductions which concern those forms and in some way are important, either from practical utility or theoretical interest. Here I am speaking of the science as it in fact exists. A theoretical definition of mathematics must include in its scope any deductions depending on the mere forms of propositions. But, of course no one would wish to develop that part of mathematics which in no sense is of importance.

This hasty summary of logical ideas suggests some reflections. The question arises, How many forms of propositions are there? The answer is, An unending number. The reason for the supposed sterility of logical science can thus be discerned. Aristotle founded the science by conceiving the idea of the form of a proposition, and by conceiving deduction as taking place in virtue of the forms. But he confined propositions to four forms, now named A, I, E, O. So long as logicians were obsessed by this unfortunate restriction, real progress was impossible. Again, in their theory of form, both Aristotle and subsequent logicians came very near-to the theory of the logical variable. But to come very near to a true theory, and to grasp its precise application, are two very different things, as the history of science teaches us. Everything of importance has been said before by somebody who did not discover it.

Again, one reason why logical deductions are not obvious is, that logical form is not a subject which ordinarily enters into thought. Commonsense deduction probably moves by blind instinct from concrete proposition to concrete proposition, guided by some habitual association of ideas. Thus commonsense fails in the presence of a wealth of material.

A more important question is the relation of induction, based on observation, to deductive logic. There is a tradition of opposition between adherents of induction and of deduction. In my view, it would be just as sensible for the two ends of a worm to quarrel. Both observation and deduction are necessary for any knowledge worth having. We cannot get at an inductive law without having recourse to a propositional function. For example, take the statement of observed fact,

> This body is mercury, and its specific heat
> is 0·033.

The propositional function is formed,

> Either x is not mercury, or its specific heat
> is 0·033.

The inductive law is the assumption of the truth of the general proposition, that the above propositional function is true for every value of x in the relevant type.

But it is objected that this process and its consequences are so simple that an elaborate science is out of place. In the same way, a British sailor knows the salt sea when he sails over it. What, then, is the use of an elaborate chemical analysis of sea-water? There is the general answer, that you cannot know too much of methods which you always employ; and there is the special answer, that logical forms and logical implications are not so very simple, and that the whole of mathematics is evidence to this effect.

One great use of the study of logical method is not in the region of elaborate deduction, but to guide us in the study of the formation of the main concepts of science. Consider geometry, for example. What are the points which compose space? Euclid tells us that they are without parts and without magnitude. But how is the notion of a point derived from the sense-perceptions from which science starts ? Certainly points are not direct deliverances of the senses. Here and there we may see or unpleasantly feel something suggestive of a point. But this is a rare phenomenon, and certainly does not warrant the conception of space as composed of points. Our knowledge of space properties is not based on any observations of relations between points. It arises from experience of relations between bodies. Now a fundamental space-relation between bodies is that one body may be part of another. We are tempted to define the " whole and part " relation by saying that the points occupied by the part are some of the points occupied by the whole. But " whole and part " being more fundamental than the notion of " point," this definition is really circular and vicious.

We accordingly ask whether any other definition of " spatial whole and part " can be given. I think that it can be done in this way, though, if I be mistaken, it is unessential to my general argument. We have come to the conclusion that an extended body is nothing else than the class of perception of it by all its percipients, actual or ideal. Of course, it is not any class of perceptions, but a certain definite sort of class which I have not defined here, except by the vicious

K

method of saying that they are perceptions of body. Now, the perceptions of a part of a body are among the perceptions which compose the whole body. Thus two bodies a and b are both classes of perceptions; and b is part of a when the class which is b is contained in the class which is a. It immediately follows from the logical form of this definition that if b is part of a, and c is part of b, then c is part of a. Thus the relation " whole to part " is transitive. Again, it will be convenient to allow that a body is part of itself. This is a mere question of how you draw the definition. With this understanding, the relation is reflexive. Finally, if a is part of b, and b is part of a, then a and b must be identical. These properties of " whole and part " are not fresh assumptions, they follow from the logical form of our definition.

One assumption has to be made if we assume the ideal infinite divisibility of space. Namely, we assume that every class of perceptions which is an extended body contains other classes of perceptions which are extended bodies diverse from itself. This assumption makes rather a large draft on the theory of ideal perceptions. Geometry vanishes unless in some form you make it. The assumption is not peculiar to my exposition.

It is then possible to define what we mean by

a point. A point is the class of extended objects which, in ordinary language, contain that point. The definition, without presupposing the idea of a point, is rather elaborate, and I have not now time for its statement.

The advantage of introducing points into geometry is the simplicity of the logical expression of their mutual relations. For science, simplicity of definition is of slight importance, but simplicity of mutual relations is essential. Another example of this law is the way physicists and chemists have dissolved the simple idea of an extended body, say of a chair, which a child understands, into a bewildering notion of a complex dance of molecules and atoms and electrons and waves of light. They have thereby gained notions with simpler logical relations.

Space as thus conceived is the exact formulation of the properties of the apparent space of the commonsense world of experience. It is not necessarily the best mode of conceiving the space of the physicist. The one essential requisite is that the correspondence between the common-sense world in its space and the physicists' world in its space should be definite and reciprocal.

I will now break off the exposition of the function of logic in connection with the science of natural phenomena. I have endeavoured to exhibit it as the organising principle, analysing the derivation of the concepts from the immediate phenomena, examining the structure of the general propositions which are the assumed laws of nature, establishing their relations to each other in respect to reciprocal implications, deducing the phenomena we may expect under given circumstances.

Logic, properly used, does not shackle thought. It gives freedom, and above all, boldness. Illogical thought hesitates to draw conclusions, because it never knows either what it means, or what it assumes, or how far it trusts its own assumptions, or what will be the effect of any modification of assumptions. Also the mind untrained in that part of constructive logic which is relevant to the subject in hand will be ignorant of the sort of conclusions which follow from various sorts of assumptions, and will be correspondingly dull in divining the inductive laws. The fundamental training in this relevant logic is, undoubtedly, to ponder with an active mind over the known facts of the case, directly observed. But where elaborate deductions are possible, this mental activity requires for its full exercise the direct study of the abstract logical relations. This is applied mathematics.

Neither logic without observation, nor observation without logic, can move one step in the formation of science. We may conceive humanity as engaged in an internecine conflict between youth and age. Youth is not defined by years but by the creative impulse to make something. The aged are those who, before all things, desire not to make a mistake. Logic is the olive branch from the old to the young, the wand which in the hands of youth has the magic property of creating science.

CHAPTER VII

THE ANATOMY OF SOME SCIENTIFIC IDEAS

I. Fact

THE characteristic of physical science is, that it ignores all judgments of value: for example, æsthetic or moral judgments. It is purely matter-of-fact, and this is the sense in which we must interpret the sonorous phrase, " Man, the servant and the minister of Nature."

The sphere of thought which is thus left is even then too wide for physical science. It would include Ontology, namely, the determination of the nature of what truly exists; in other words, Metaphysics. From an abstract point of view this exclusion of metaphysical inquiry is a pity. Such an inquiry is a necessary critique of the worth of science, to tell us what it all comes to. The reasons for its careful separation from scientific thought are purely practical; namely, because we can agree about science—after due debate—whereas in respect to metaphysics debate has hitherto accentuated disagreement. These characteristics of science and metaphysics were unexpected in the early days of civilised thought. The Greeks thought that metaphysics was easier than physics, and tended to deduce scientific principles from *a priori* conceptions of the nature of things. They were restrained in this disastrous tendency by their vivid naturalism, their delight in first-hand perception. Mediæval Europe shared the tendency without the restraint. It is possible that some distant generations may arrive at unanimous conclusions on ontological questions, whereas scientific progress may have led to ingrained opposing veins of thought which can neither be reconciled nor abandoned. In such times metaphysics and physical science will exchange their rôles. Meanwhile we must take the case as we find it.

But a problem remains. How can mankind agree about science without a preliminary determination of what really is? The answer must be found in an analysis of the facts which form the field of scientific activity. Mankind perceives, and finds itself thinking about its perceptions. It is the thought that matters and not that element of perception which is not thought. When the immediate judgment has been formed— Hullo, red !—it does not matter if we can imagine that in other circumstances—in better circumstances, perhaps—the judgment would have been —Hullo, blue !—or even—Hullo, nothing ! For all intents and purposes, at the time it was red.

Everything else is hypothetical reconstruction. The field of physical science is composed of these primary thoughts, and of thoughts about these thoughts.

But—to avoid confusion—a false simplicity has been introduced above into the example given of a primary perceptive thought. " Hullo, red ! " is not really a primary perceptive thought, though it often is the first thought which finds verbal expression even silently in the mind. Nothing is in isolation. The perception of red is of a red object in its relations to the whole content of the perceiving consciousness.

Among the most easily analysed of such relations are the space relations. Again the red object is in immediate perception nothing else than a red object. It is better termed an " object of redness." Thus a better-approximation to an immediate perceptive judgment is, " Hullo, object of redness there ! " But, of course, in this formulation other more complex relations are omitted.

This tendency towards a false simplicity in scientific analysis, to an excessive abstraction, to an over-universalising of universals, is derived from the earlier metaphysical stage. It arises from the implicit belief that we are endeavouring to qualify the real with appropriate adjectives. In conformity with this tendency we think, " this real thing is red." Whereas our true goal is to make explicit our perception of the apparent in terms of its relations. What we perceive is redness related to other apparents. Our object is the analysis of the relations.

One aim of science is the harmony of thought, that is, to secure that judgments which are logical contraries should not be thought-expressions of consciousness. Another aim is the extension of such harmonised thought.

Some thoughts arise directly from sense-presentation, and are part of the state of consciousness which is perception. Such a thought is, " An object of redness is there." But in general the thought is not verbal, but is a direct apprehension of qualities and relations within the content of consciousness.

Amid such thoughts there can be no lack of harmony. For direct apprehension is in its essence unique, and it is impossible to apprehend an object as both red and blue. Subsequently it may be judged that if other elements of the consciousness had been different, the apprehension would have been of a blue object. Then —under certain circumstances—the original apprehension will be called an error. But for all that the fact remains, there was an apprehension of a red object.

When we speak of sense-presentation, we mean these primary thoughts essentially involved in its perception. But there are thoughts about thoughts, and thoughts derived from other thoughts. These are secondary thoughts. At this point it is well explicitly to discriminate between an actual thought-expression, namely, a judgment actually made, and a mere proposition which is a hypothetical thought-expression, namely, an imagined possibility of thought-expression. Note that the actual complete thought-content of the consciousness is explicitly neither affirmed or denied. It is just what *is* thought. Thus, to think " two and two make four " is distinct from affirming that two and two make four. In the first case the proposition is the thought-expression, in the second case the affirmation of the proposition is the thought-expression, and the proposition has been degraded to a mere proposition, namely, to a hypothetical thought-expression which is reflected upon.

A distinction is sometimes made between facts and thoughts. So far as physical science is concerned, the facts are thoughts, and thoughts are facts. Namely, the facts of sense-presentation as they affect science are those elements in the immediate apprehensions which are thoughts. Also, actual thought-expressions, primary or secondary, are the material facts which science interprets.

The distinction that facts are given, but thoughts are free, is not absolute. We can select and modify our sense-presentation, so that facts

—in the narrower sense of immediate apprehension of sense-presentation—are to some degree subject to volition. Again, our stream of thought-expression is only partially modified by explicit volition. We can choose our physical experience, and we find ourselves thinking; namely, on the one hand there is selection amid the dominant necessity of sense, and on the other hand, the thought-content of consciousness (so far as secondary thoughts are concerned) is not wholly constituted by the selection of will.

Thus, on the whole there is a large primary region of secondary thought, as well as of the primary thoughts of sense-presentation, which is given in type. That is the way in which we do think of things, not wholly from any abstract necessity, so far as we know, but because we have inherited the method from an environment. It is the way we find ourselves thinking, a way which can only be fundamentally laid aside by an immense effort, and then only for isolated short periods of time. This is what I have called the " whole apparatus of commonsense thought."

It is this body of thought which is assumed in science. It is a way of thinking rather than a set of axioms. It is, in fact, the set of concepts which commonsense has found useful in sorting out human experience. It is modified in detail, but assumed in gross. The explanations of science are directed to finding conceptions and propositions concerning nature which explain the importance of these commonsense notions. For example, a chair is a commonsense notion, molecules and electrons explain our vision of chairs.

Now science aims at harmonising our reflective and derivative thoughts with the primary thoughts involved in the immediate apprehension of sense-presentation. It also aims at producing such derivative thoughts, logically knit together. This is scientific theory; and the harmony to be achieved is the agreement of theory with observation, which is the apprehension of sense-presentation.

Thus there is a two-fold scientific aim : (1) the production of theory which agrees with experience; and (2) the explanation of commonsense concepts of nature, at least in their main outlines. This explanation consists in the preservation of the concepts in a scientific theory of harmonised thought.

It is not asserted that this is what scientists in the past meant to achieve, or thought that they could achieve. It is suggested as the actual result of scientific effort, so far as that effort has had any measure of success. In short, we are here discussing the natural history of ideas and not volitions of scientists.

II. Objects

We perceive things in space. For example, among such things are dogs, chairs, curtains, drops of water, gusts of air, flames, rainbows, chimes of bells, odours, aches and pains. There is a scientific explanation of the origin of these perceptions. This explanation is given in terms of molecules, atoms, electrons, and their mutual relations, in particular of their space-relations, and waves of disturbance of these space-relations which are propagated through space. The primary elements of the scientific explanation—molecules, etc.—are not the things directly perceived. For example, we do not perceive a wave of light; the sensation of sight is the resultant effect of the impact of millions of such waves through a stretch of time. Thus the object directly perceived corresponds to a series of events in the physical world, events which are prolonged through a stretch of time. Nor is it true that a perceived object always corresponds to the same group of molecules. After a few years we recognise the same cat, but we are thereby related to different molecules.

Again, neglecting for a moment the scientific explanation, the perceived object is largely the supposition of our imagination. When we recognised the cat, we also recognised that it was glad to see us. But we merely heard its mewing, saw it arch its back, and felt it rubbing itself against us. We must distinguish, therefore, between the many direct objects of sense, and the single indirect object of thought which is the cat.

Thus, when we say that we perceived the cat and understood its feelings, we mean that we heard a sense-object of sound, that we saw a sense-object of sight, that we felt a sense-object of touch, and that we thought of a cat and imagined its feelings.

Sense-objects are correlated by time-relations and space-relations. Three simultaneous sense-objects which are also spatially coincident, are combined by thought into the perception of one cat. Such combination of sense-objects is an instinctive immediate judgment in general without effort of reasoning. Sometimes only one sense-object is present. For example, we hear mewing and say there must be a cat in the room. The transition from the sense-object to the cat has then been made, by deliberate ratiocination. Even the concurrence of sense-objects may provoke such a self-conscious effort. For example, in the dark we feel something, and hear mewing from the same place, and think, Surely this is a cat. Sight is more bold; when we see a cat, we do not think further. We identify the sight with the cat, whereas the cat and the mew are separate. But such immediate identification of a sight object and an object of thought may lead to error; the birds pecked at the grapes of Apelles.

A single sense-object is a complex entity. The sight-object of a tile on the hearth may remain unchanged as we watch it in a steady light, remaining ourselves unchanged in position. Even then it is prolonged in time, and has parts in space. Also it is somewhat arbitrarily distinguished from a larger whole of which it forms part. But the glancing fire-light and a change in our position alters the sight-object. We judge that the tile thought-object remains unchanged. The sight-object of the coal on the fire gradually modifies, though within short intervals it remains unchanged. We judge that the coal thought-object is changing. The flame is never the same, and its shape is only vaguely distinguishable.

We conclude that a single self-identical sight-object is already a phantasy of thought. Consider the unchanging sight-object of the tile, as we remain still in a steady light. Now a sense-object perceived at one time is a distinct object from a sense-object seen at another time. Thus the sight of the tile at noon is distinct from its sight at 12.30. But there is no such thing as a sense-object at an instant. As we stare at the tile, a minute, or a second, or a tenth of a second, has flown by : essentially there is a duration. There is a stream of sight, and we can distinguish its parts. But the parts also are streams, and it is only in thought that the stream separates into a succession of elements. The stream may be " steady " as in the case of the unchanging sight-tile, or may be " turbulent " as in the case of the glancing sight-flame. In either case a sight-object is some arbitrarily small part of the stream.

Again, the stream which forms the succession of sight-tiles is merely a distinguishable part of the whole stream of sight-presentation.

So, finally, we conceive ourselves each experiencing a complete time-flux (or stream) of sense-presentation. This stream is distinguishable into parts. The grounds of distinction are differences of sense—including within that term, differences of types of sense, and differences of quality and of intensity within the same type of sense—and differences of time-relations, and differences of space-relations. Also the parts are not mutually exclusive and exist in unbounded variety.

The time-relation between the parts raises the questions of memory and recognition, subjects too complex for discussion here. One remark must be made. If it be admitted, as stated above, that we live in durations and not in instants, namely, that the present essentially occupies a stretch of time, the distinction between memory and immediate presentation cannot be quite fundamental; for always we have with us the fading present as it becomes the immediate past. This region of our consciousness is neither pure memory nor pure immediate presentation. Anyhow, memory is also a presentation in consciousness.

Another point is to be noted in connection with memory. There is no directly perceived time-relation between a present event and a past event. The present event is only related to the memory of the past event. But the memory of a past event is itself a present element in consciousness. We assert the principle that directly perceived relations can only exist between elements of consciousness, both in that present during which the perception occurs. All other relations between elements of perception are inferential constructions. It thus becomes necessary to explain how the time stream of events establishes itself in thought, and how the apparent world fails to collapse into one single present. The solution of the difficulty is arrived at by observing that the present is itself a duration, and therefore includes directly perceived time-relations between events contained within it. In other words we put the present on the same footing as the past and the future in respect to the inclusion within it of antecedent and succeeding events, so that past, present, and future are in this respect exactly analogous

L

ideas. Thus there will be two events a and b, both in the same present, but the event a will be directly perceived to precede the event b. Again time flows on, and the event a fades into the past, and in the new present duration events b and c occur, event b preceding event c, also in the same present duration there is the memory of the time-relation between a and b. Then by an inferential construction the event a in the past precedes the event c in the present. By proceeding according to this principle the time-relations between elements of consciousness, not in the same present, are established. The method of procedure here explained is a first example of what we will call the Principle of Aggregation. This is one of the fundamental principles of mental construction according to which our conception of the external physical world is constructed. Other examples will later on be met with.

The space-relations between the parts are confused and fluctuating, and in general lack determinate precision. The master-key by which we confine our attention to such parts as possess mutual relations sufficiently simple for our intellects to consider is the principle of convergence to simplicity with diminution of extent. We will call it the " principle of convergence." This principle extends throughout the whole field of sense-presentation.

The first application of the principle occurs in respect to time. The shorter the stretch of time, the simpler are the aspects of the sense-presentation contained within it. The perplexing effects of change are diminished and in many cases can be neglected. Nature has restricted the acts of thought which endeavour to realise the content of the present, to stretches of time sufficiently short to secure this static simplicity over the greater part of the sense-stream.

Spatial relations become simplified within the approximately static sense-world of the short time. A further simplicity is gained by partitioning this static world into parts of restricted space-content. The various parts thus obtained have simpler mutual space-relations, and again the principle of convergence holds.

Finally, the last simplicity is obtained by partitioning the parts, already restricted as to space and time, into further parts characterised by homogeneity in type of sense, and homogeneity in quality and intensity of sense. These three processes of restriction yield, finally, the sense-objects which have been mentioned above. Thus the sense-object is the result of an active process of discrimination made in virtue of the principle of convergence. It is the result of the quest for simplicity of relations within the complete stream of sense-presentation.

The thought-objects of perception are instances

of a fundamental law of nature, the law of objective stability. It is the law of the coherence of sense-objects. This law of stability has an application to time and an application to space; also it must be applied in conjunction with that other law, the principle of convergence to simplicity from which sense-objects are derived.

Some composite partial streams of sense-presentation can be distinguished with the following characteristics : (1) the time-succession of sense-objects, belonging to a single sense, involved in any such a composite partial stream, is composed of very similar objects whose modifications increase only gradually, and thus forms a homogeneous component stream within the composite stream; (2) the space-relations of those sense-objects (of various senses) of such a composite stream which are confined within any sufficiently short time are identical so far as they are definitely apprehended, and thus these various component streams, each homogeneous, "cohere" to form the whole composite partial stream; (3) there are other sense-presentations occurring in association with that composite partial stream which can be determined by rules derived from analogous composite partial streams, with other space and time relations, provided that the analogy be sufficiently close. Call these the "associated sense-presentations." A partial stream of this sort, viewed as a whole, is here called a " first crude thought-object of perception."

For example, we look at an orange for half a minute, handle it, and smell it, note its position in the fruit-basket, and then turn away. The stream of sense-presentation of the orange during that half-minute is a first crude thought-object of perception. Among the associated sense presentations are those of the fruit-basket which we conceive as supporting the orange.

The essential ground of the association of sense-objects of various types, perceived within one short duration, into a first crude thought-object of perception is the coincidence of their space-relations, that is, in general an approximate coincidence of such relations perhaps only vaguely apprehended. Thus coincident space-relations associate sense-objects into a first crude thought-object, and diverse space-relations dissociate sense-objects from aggregation into a first crude thought-object. In respect to some groups of sense-objects the association may be an immediate judgment devoid of all inference, so that the primary perceptual thought is that of the first crude thought-object, and the separate sense-objects are the result of reflective analysis acting on memory. For example sense-objects of sight and sense-objects of touch are often thus primarily associated and only secondarily dissociated in thought. But sometimes the association is wavering and indeterminate, for example, that between the sound-object of the mew of the cat and the sight-object of the cat. Thus to sum up, the partial stream of sense-perceptions coalesces into that first crude thought-object of perception which is the momentary cat because the sense-perceptions belonging to this stream are in the same place, but equally it would be true to say that they are in the same place because they belong to the same momentary cat. This analysis of the complete stream of sense-presentation in any small present duration into a variety of first crude thought-objects only partially fits the facts; for one reason because many sense-objects, such as sound for instance, have vague and indeterminate space-relations, for example vaguely those space-relations which we associate with our organs of sense and also vaguely those of the origin from which (in the scientific explanation) they proceed.

The procedure by which the orange of half a minute is elaborated into the orange in the ordinary sense of the term involves in addition the two principles of aggregation and of hypothetical sense-presentation.

The principle of aggregation, as here employed, takes the form that many distinct first crude thought-objects of perception are conceived as one thought-object of perception, if the many partial streams forming these objects are sufficiently analogous, if their times of occurrence are distinct, and if the associated sense-presentations are sufficiently analogous.

For example, after leaving the orange, in five minutes we return. A new first crude thought-object of perception presents itself to us, indistinguishable from the half-minute orange we previously experienced; it is in the same fruit-basket. We aggregate the two presentations of an orange into the same orange. By such aggregations we obtain " second crude thought-objects of perception." But however far we can proceed with aggregation of this type, the orange is more than that. For example, what do we mean when we say, The orange is in the cupboard, if Tom has not eaten it?

The world of present fact is more than a stream of sense-presentation. We find ourselves with emotions, volitions, imaginations, conceptions, and judgments. No factor which enters into consciousness is by itself or even can exist in isolation. We are analysing certain relations between sense-presentation and other factors of consciousness. Hitherto we have taken into account merely the factors of concept and judgment. Imagination is necessary to complete the orange, namely, the imagination of hypothetical sense-presentations. It is beside the point to argue whether we ought to have such imaginations, or to discuss what are the metaphysical truths concerning reality to which they correspond. We are here only concerned with the fact that such imaginations exist and essentially enter into the formation of the concepts of the thought-objects of perception which are the first data of science. We conceive the orange as a permanent collection of sense-presentations existing as if they were an actual element in our consciousness, which they are not. The orange is thus conceived as in the cupboard with its shape, odour, colour, and other qualities. Namely, we imagine hypothetical possibilities of sense-presentation, and conceive their want of actuality in our consciousness as immaterial to their existence in fact. The fact which is essential for science is our conception; its meaning in regard to the metaphysics of reality is of no scientific importance, so far as physical science is concerned.

The orange completed in this way is the thought-object of perception.

It must be remembered that the judgments and concepts arising in the formation of thought-objects of perception are in the main instinctive judgments, and instinctive concepts, and are not concepts and judgments consciously sought for and consciously criticised before adoption. Their adoption is facilitated by and interwoven with the expectation of the future in which the hypothetical passes into the actual, and also with the further judgment of the existence of other consciousnesses, so that much that is hypothetical to one consciousness is judged to be actual to others.

The thought-object of perception is, in fact, a device to make plain to our reflective consciousness relations which hold within the complete stream of sense-presentation. Concerning the utility of this weapon there can be no question; it is the rock upon which the whole structure of commonsense thought is erected. But when we consider the limits of its application the evidence is confused. A great part of our sense-presentation can be construed as perception of various persistent thought-objects. But hardly at any time can the sense-presentations be construed wholly in that way. Sights lend themselves easily to this construction, but sight can be baffled : for example, consider reflections in looking-glasses, apparently bent sticks half in and half out of water, rainbows, brilliant patches of light which conceal the object from which they emanate, and many analogous phenomena. Sound is more difficult; it tends largely to disengage itself from any such object. For example, we see the bell, but we hear the sound which comes from the bell; yet we also say that we hear the bell. Again, a toothache is largely by itself, and is only indirectly a perception of the nerve of the tooth. Illustrations to the same effect can be accumulated from every type of sensation.

Another difficulty arises from the fact of change. The thought-object is conceived as one thing, wholly actual at each instant. But since the meat has been bought it has been cooked, the grass grows and then withers, the coal burns in the fire, the pyramids of Egypt remain unchanged for ages, but even the pyramids are not wholly unchanged. The difficulty of change is merely evaded by affixing a technical Latin name to a supposed logical fallacy. A slight cooking leaves the meat the same object, but two days in the oven burns it to a cinder. When does the meat cease to be? Now the chief use of the thought-object is the concept of it as one thing, here and now, which later can be recognised, there and then. This concept applies sufficiently well to most things for short times, and to many things for long times. But sense-presentation as a whole entirely refuses to be patient of the concept.

We have now come to the reflective region of explanation, which is science.

A great part of the difficulty is at once removed by applying the principle of convergence to simplicity. We habitually make our thought-objects too large; we should think in smaller parts. For example, the Sphinx has changed by its nose becoming chipped, but by proper inquiry we could find the missing part in some private house of Western Europe or Northern America. Thus, either part, the rest of the Sphinx or the chip, regains its permanence. Furthermore, we enlarge this explanation by conceiving parts so small that they can only be observed under the most favourable circumstances. This is a wide extension of the principle of convergence in its application to nature; but it is a principle amply supported by the history of exact observation.

Thus, change in thought-objects of perception is largely explained as a disintegration into smaller parts, themselves thought-objects of perception. The thought-objects of perception which are presupposed in the common thought of civilised beings are almost wholly hypothetical. The material universe is largely a concept of the imagination which rests on a slender basis of direct sense-presentation. But none the less it is a fact; for it is a fact that actually we imagine it. Thus it is actual in our consciousness just as sense-presentation also is actual there. The effort of reflective criticism is to make these two factors in our consciousness agree where they are related, namely, to construe our sense-presentation as actual realisation of the hypothetical thought-objects of perception.

The wholesale employment of purely hypothetical thought-objects of perception enables science to explain some of the stray sense-objects which cannot be construed as perceptions of a thought-object of perception : for example, sounds. But the phenomena as a whole defy explanation on these lines until a further fundamental step is taken, which transforms the whole concept of the material universe. Namely, the thought-object of perception is superseded by the thought-object of science.

The thought-objects of science are molecules, atoms, and electrons. The peculiarity of these objects is that they have shed all the qualities which are capable of direct sense-representation in consciousness. They are known to us only by their associated phenomena, namely, series of events in which they are implicated are represented in our consciousness by sense-presentations. In this way, the thought-objects of science are conceived as the causes of sense-representation. The transition from thought-objects of perception to thought-objects of science is decently veiled by an elaborate theory concerning primary and secondary qualities of bodies.

This device, by which sense-presentations are represented in thought as our perception of events in which thought-objects of science are implicated, is the fundamental means by which a bridge is formed between the fluid vagueness of sense and the exact definition of thought. In thought a proposition is either true or false, an entity is exactly what it is, and relations between entities are expressible (in idea) by definite propositions about distinctly conceived entities. Sense-perception knows none of these things, except by courtesy. Accuracy essentially collapses at some stage of inquiry.

III. Time and Space

Recapitulation.—Relations of time and relations of space hold between sense-objects of perception. These sense-objects are distinguished as separate objects by the recognition of either (1) differences of sense-content, or (2) time-relations between them other than simultaneity, or (3) space-relations between them other than coincidence. Thus sense-objects arise from the recognition of contrast within the complete stream of sense-presentation, namely, from the recognition of the objects as related terms, by relations which contrast them. Differences of sense-content are infinitely complex in their variety. Their analysis under the heading of general ideas is the unending task of physical science. Time-relations and space-relations are comparatively simple, and the general ideas according to which their analysis should proceed are obvious.

This simplicity of time and space is perhaps the reason why thought chooses them as the permanent ground for objectival distinction, throwing the various sense-objects thus obtainable into one heap, as a first crude thought-object of perception, and thence, as described above, obtaining a thought-object of perception. Thus a thought-object of perception conceived as in the present of a short duration is a first crude thought-object of perception either actual or hypothetical. Such a thought-object of perception, confined within a short duration, takes on the space-relations of its component sense-objects within that same duration. Accordingly thought-objects of perception, conceived in their whole extents, have to each other the time-relationships of their complete existences, and within any small duration have to each other the space-relationships of their component sense-objects which lie within that duration.

Relations bind together : thus thought-objects of perception are connected in time and in space. The genesis of the objectival analysis of sense-presentation is the recognition of sense-objects as distinct terms in time-relations and space-relations : thus thought-objects of perception are separated by time and by space.

Whole and Part.—A sense-object is part of the complete stream of presentation. This concept of being a part is merely the statement of the relation of the sense-object to the complete sense-presentation for that consciousness. Also a sense-object can be part of another sense-object. It can be a part in two ways, namely, a part in time and a part in space. It seems probable that both these concepts of time-part and space-part are fundamental; that is, are concepts expressing relations which are directly presented to us, and are not concepts about concepts. In that case no further definition of the actual presentation is possible. It may even then be possible to define an adequate criterion of the occurrence of such a presentation. For example, adopting for the moment a realist metaphysic as to the existence of the physical world of molecules and electrons, the vision of a chair as occurring for some definite person at some definite time is essentially indefinable. It is his vision, though each of us guesses that it must be uncommonly like our vision under analogous circumstances. But the existence of the definable molecules and waves of light in certain definable relations to his bodily organs of sense, his body also being in a certain definable state, forms an adequate criterion of the occurrence of the vision, a criterion which is accepted in Courts of Law and for physical science is tacitly substituted for the vision.

The connection between the relations " whole and part " and " all and some " is intimate. It can be explained thus so far as concerns directly presented sense-objects. Call two sense-objects

" separated " if there is no third sense-object which is a part of both of them. Then an object A is composed of the two objects B and C, if (1) B and C, are both parts of A, (2) B and C are separated, and (3) there is no part of A which is separated both from B and from C. In such a case the class α which is composed of the two objects B and C is often substituted in thought for the sense-object A. But this process presupposes the fundamental relation " whole and part." Conversely the objects B and C may be actual sense-objects, but the sense-object A which corresponds to the class α may remain hypothetical. For example, the round world on which we live remains a conception corresponding to no single sense-object at any time presented in any human being's consciousness.

It is possible, however, that some mode of conceiving the whole-and-part relation between extended objects as the all-and-some relation of logical classes can be found. But in this case the extended objects as here conceived cannot be the true sense-objects which are present to consciousness. For as here conceived a part of a sense-object is another sense-object of the same type; and therefore one sense-object cannot be a class of other sense-objects, just as a tea-spoon cannot be a class of other tea-spoons. The ordinary way in thought by which whole-and-part is reduced to all-and-some is by the device of points, namely, the part of an object occupies some of the points occupied by the whole object. If any one holds that in his consciousness the sense-presentation is a presentation of point-objects, and that an extended object is merely a class of such point-objects collected together in thought, then this ordinary method is completely satisfactory. We shall proceed on the assumption that this conception of directly perceived point-objects has no relation to the facts.

In the preceding address on " The Organisation of Thought," another mode is suggested. But this method would apply only to the thought-object of perception, and has no reference to the primary sense-objects here considered. Accordingly it must reckon as a subordinate device for a later stage of thought.

Thus the point-object in time and the point-object in space, and the double point-object both in time and space, must be conceived as intellectual constructions. The fundamental fact is the sense-object, extended both in time and space, with the fundamental relation of whole-to-part to other such objects, and subject to the law of convergence to simplicity as we proceed in thought through a series of successively contained parts.

The relation whole-to-part is a temporal or spatial relation, and is therefore primarily a

M

relation holding between sense-objects of perception, and it is only derivatively ascribed to the thought-objects of perception of which they are components. More generally, space and time relations hold primarily between sense-objects of perception and derivatively between thought-objects of perception.

Definition of Points.—The genesis of points of time and of space can now be studied. We must distinguish (1) sense-time and sense-space, and (2) thought-time of perception and thought-space of perception.

Sense-time and sense-space are the actually observed time-relations and space-relations between sense-objects. Sense-time and sense-space have no points except, perhaps, a few sparse instances, sufficient to suggest the logical idea; also, sense-time and sense-space are discontinuous and fragmentary.

Thought-time of perception and thought-space of perception are the time and space relations which hold between thought-objects of perception. Thought-time of perception and thought-space of perception are each continuous. By "continuous" is here meant that all thought-objects of perception have to each other a time (or space) relation.

The origin of points is the effort to take full advantage of the principle of convergence to simplicity. In so far as this principle does not apply, a point is merely a cumbrous way of directing attention to a set of relations between a certain set of thought-objects of perception, which set of relations, though actual so far as a thought-object is actual, is (under this supposition) of no particular importance. Thus the proved importance in physical science of the concepts of points in time and points in space is a tribute to the wide applicability of this principle of convergence.

Euclid defines a point as without parts and without magnitude. In modern language a point is often described as an ideal limit by indefinitely continuing the process of diminishing a volume (or area). Points as thus conceived are often called convenient fictions. This language is ambiguous. What is meant by a fiction? If it means a conception which does not correspond to any fact, there is some difficulty in understanding how it can be of any use in physical science. For example, the fiction of a red man in a green coat inhabiting the moon can never be of the slightest scientific service, simply because—as we may presume—it corresponds to no fact. By calling the concept of points a convenient fiction, it must be meant that the concept does correspond to some important facts. It is, then, requisite, in the place of such vague allusiveness, to explain exactly what are the facts to which the concept corresponds.

We are not much helped by explaining that a point is an ideal limit. What is a limit? The idea of a limit has a precise meaning in the theory of series, and in the theory of the values of functions; but neither of these meanings apply here. It may be observed that, before the ordinary mathematical meanings of limit had received a precise explanation, the idea of a point as a limit might be considered as one among other examples of an idea only to be apprehended by direct intuition. This view is not now open to us. Thus, again, we are confronted with the question : What are the precise properties meant when a point is described as an ideal limit? The discussion which now follows is an attempt to express the concept of a point in terms of thought-objects of perception related together by the whole-and-part relation, considered either as a time-relation or as a space-relation. If it is so preferred, it may be considered that the discussion is directed towards a precise elucidation of the term " ideal limit " as often used in this connection.

The subsequent explanations can be made easier to follow by a small piece of symbolism: Let aEb mean that " b is part of a." We need not decide whether we are talking of time-parts or space-parts, but whichever choice is supposed to be made must be conceived as adhered to throughout any connected discussion. The symbol E may be considered as the initial letter of " encloses," so we read " aEb " as " a encloses b." Again the " field of E " is the set of things which either enclose or are enclosed, *i. e.* everything " a," which is such that x can be found so that either aEx or xEa. A member of the field of E is called " an enclosure-object."

Now, we assume that this relation of whole-to-part, which in the future we will call " enclosure," always satisfies the conditions in that the relation E is (1) transitive, (2) asymmetrical, and (3) with its domain including its converse domain.

These four conditions deserve some slight consideration; only the first two of them embody hypotheses which enter vitally into the reasoning.

Condition (1) may be stated as the condition that aEb and bEc always implies aEc. The fact that an entity b can be found such that aEb and bEc may be conceived as a relation between a and c. It is natural to write E^2 for this relation. Thus the condition is now written: If aE^2c, then aEc. This can be still otherwise expressed by saying that the relation E^2 implies, whenever it holds, that the relation E also holds.

Condition (2) is partly a mere question of trivial definition, and partly a substantial assumption. The asymmetrical relation (E) is such that aEb and bEa can never hold simultaneously. This property splits up into two parts : (1) that no instance of aEb and bEa and " a diverse from b," can occur, and (2) that aEa cannot occur. The first part is a substantial assumption, the second part (so far as we are concerned) reduces to the trivial convention that we shall not consider an object as part of itself, but will confine attention to " proper parts."

Condition (3) means that aEb always implies that c can be found such that bEc. This condition, taken in conjunction with the fact that we are only considering proper parts, is the assertion of the principle of the indefinite divisibility of extended objects, both in space and in time.

An indivisible part will lack duration in time, and extension in space, and is thus an entity of essentially a different character to a divisible part. If we admit such indivisibles as the only true sense-objects, our subsequent procedure is an unnecessary elaboration.

It will be found that a fourth condition is necessary owing to logical difficulties connected with the theory of an infinite number of choices. It will not be necessary for us to enter further on this question, which involves difficult considerations of abstract logic. The outcome is, that apart from hypothesis we cannot prove the existence of the sets, each containing an infinite number of objects, which are here called points, as will be explained immediately.

Now consider a set of enclosure objects which

is such that (1) of any two of its members one encloses the other, and (2) there is no member which is enclosed by all the others, and (3) there is no enclosure-object, not a member of the set which is enclosed by every member of the set. Call such a set a " convergent set of enclosure-objects." As we pass along the series from larger to smaller members, evidently we converge towards an ideal simplicity to any degree of approximation to which we like to proceed, and the series as a whole embodies the complete ideal along that route of approximation. In fact, to repeat, the series is a *route of approximation.*

We have now to inquire if the principle of convergence to simplicity may be expected to yield the same type of simplicity for every such convergent route. The answer is, as we might expect, namely, that this depends upon the nature of the properties which are to be simplified.

For example, consider the application to time. Now, time is one-dimensional; so when this property of one-dimensionality has been expressed by the proper conditions, not here stated, a convergent set of enclosure-objects must, considered as a route of approximation, exhibit the properties of one unique instant of time, as ordinarily conceived by the euclidean definition. Accordingly, whatever simplicity is to be achieved by the application to time of the principle of convergence to simplicity must be exhibited among the properties of any such route of approximation.

For space, different considerations arise. Owing to its multiple dimensions, we can show that different convergent sets of enclosure-objects, indicating different routes of approximation, may exhibit convergence to different types of simplicity, some more complex than others.

For example, consider a rectangular box of height h ft., breadth b ft., and thickness c ft. Now, keep h and b constant, and let the central plane (height h, breadth b) perpendicular to the thickness be fixed, then make c diminish indefinitely. We thus obtain a convergent series of an indefinitely large number of boxes, and there is no smallest box. Thus this convergent series exhibits the route of approximation towards the type of simplicity expressed as being a plane area of height h, breadth b, and no thickness.

Again, by keeping the central line of height h fixed, and by making b and c diminish indefinitely, the series converges to the segment of a straight line of length h.

Finally, by keeping only the central point fixed, and by making h, b, and c diminish indefinitely, the series converges to a point.

Furthermore, we have introduced as yet no concept which would prevent an enclosure-object being formed of detached fragments in space. Thus we can easily imagine a convergent set which converges to a number of points in space. For example, each object of the set might be formed of two not overlapping spheres of radius r, with centres A and B. Then by diminishing r indefinitely, and keeping A and B fixed, we have convergence to the pair of points A and B.

It remains now to consider how those convergent sets which converge to a single point can be discriminated from all the other types of such sets, merely by utilising concepts founded on the relation of enclosure.

Let us name convergent sets by Greek letters; by proceeding " forward " along any such set let us understand the process of continually passing from the larger to the smaller enclosure-objects which form the set.

The convergent set a will be said to " cover " the convergent set β, if every member of a encloses some members of β. We notice that if an enclosure-object x encloses any member (y) of β, then every member of the " tail-end " of β, found by proceeding forward along β from y, must be enclosed by x. Thus if a covers β, every member of a encloses every member of the tail-end of β, starting from the largest member of β which is enclosed by that member of a.

It is possible for each of two convergent sets to cover the other. For example, let one set (a) be a set of concentric spheres converging to their centre A, and the other set (β) be a set of concentric cubes, similarly situated, converging to the same centre A. Then a and β will each cover the other.

Let two convergent sets which are such that each covers the other be called " equal."

Then it is a sufficient condition to secure that a convergent set a possesses the point type of convergence, if every convergent set covered by it is also equal to it, namely, a is a convergent set with the punctual type of convergence, if " a covers β " always implies that β covers a.

It can easily be seen by simple examples that the other types of convergence to surfaces or lines or sets of points cannot possess this property. Consider, for example, the three convergent sets of boxes in the preceding illustration, which converge respectively to a central plane, a central line in the central plane, and the central point in the central line. The first set covers the second and third sets, and the second set covers the third set, but no two of the sets are equal.

It is a more difficult question to determine whether the condition here indicated as sufficient to secure the punctual type of convergence is also necessary. The question turns on how far thought-objects of perception possess exact boundaries prior to the elaboration of exact mathematical concepts of space. If they are to be conceived as possessing such exact boundaries, then convergent sets converging to points on such boundaries must be allowed for. The procedure necessary for the specification of the complete punctual condition becomes then very elaborate,[1] and will not be considered here.

But such exact determination as is involved in the conception of an exact spatial boundary does not seem to belong to the true thought-object of perception. The ascription of an exact boundary really belongs to the transition stage of thought as it passes from the thought-object of perception to the thought-object of science. The transition from the sense-object immediately presented to the thought-object of perception is historically made in a wavering indeterminate line of thought. The definite stages here marked out simply serve to prove that a logically explicable transition is possible.

We accordingly assume that the condition laid down above to secure the punctual convergence of a convergent set of enclosure-objects is not only sufficient, but necessary.

It can be proved that, if two convergent sets of enclosure-objects are both equal to a third convergent set, they are equal to each other. Consider now any punctual convergent set (a). We want to define the " point " to which a is

[1] Cf. *Révue de Métaphysique et de Morale*, May 1916, where this question is dealt with by the author at the end of an article, " La théorie relationniste de l'espace."

a route of approximation in a way which is
neutral between a and all the convergent sets
which are equal to a.   Each of these sets is a
route of approximation to the same " point "
as a.   This definition is secured if we define the
point as the class formed by all the enclosure-
objects which belong either to a or to any convergent set which is equal to a.   Let P be this
class of enclosure-objects.   Then any convergent
set (β) which consists of enclosure-objects entirely
selected from members of the class P must be a
route of approximation to the same " point " as
does the original punctual set a; namely, provided that we choose a small enough enclosure-
object in β, we can always find a member of a
which encloses it; and provided that we choose
a small enough enclosure-object in a, we can
always find a member of β which encloses it.
Thus P only includes convergent sets of the
punctual type, and the route of approximation
indicated by any two convergent sets selected
from P converges to identical results.

The Uses of Points.—The sole use of points is
to facilitate the employment of the principle of
Convergence to Simplicity.   By this principle
some simple relations in appropriate circumstances become true, when objects are considered
which are sufficiently restricted in time or in
space.   The introduction of points enables this
principle to be carried through to its ideal limit.

For example, suppose $g\ (a,\ b,\ c)$ represents some statement concerning three enclosure-objects, $a,\ b,\ c$, which may be true if the objects are sufficiently restricted in extent. Let $A,\ B,\ C$ be three given points, then we define $g\ (A,\ B,\ C)$ to mean that *whatever* three enclosure-objects $a,\ b,\ c$ are chosen, such that a is a member of A, b of B, and c of C, it is *always possible* to find three other members of $A,\ B,\ C$, namely, x a member of A, y of B, and z of C, such that aEx, bEy, cEz, and $g\ (x,\ y,\ z)$. So by going far enough down in the tail-ends of $A,\ B,\ C$ we can always secure three objects $x,\ y,\ z$ for which $g\ (x,\ y,\ z)$ is true.

For example, let $g\ (A,\ B,\ C)$ mean "$A,\ B,\ C$ are three points in a linear row." This must be construed to mean that whatever three objects $a,\ b,\ c$ we choose, members of $A,\ B,\ C$ respectively, we can always find three objects $x,\ y,\ z$, also members of $A,\ B,\ C$ respectively, and such that a encloses x, b encloses y, c encloses z, and also such that $x,\ y,\ z$ are in a linear row.

Sometimes a double convergence is necessary, namely, a convergence of conditions as well as a convergence of objects. For example, consider the statement, "the points A and B are two feet apart." Now, the exact statement "two feet apart" does not apply to objects. For objects x and y we must substitute the statement, "the distance between x and y lies between the limits

$(2 \pm e)$ feet." Here e is some number, less than two, which we have chosen for this statement. Then the points A and B are two feet apart; if, *however we choose the number e*, whatever enclosure-objects a and b, members of A and B respectively, we consider, we can always find enclosure-objects x and y, members of A and B respectively, such that a encloses x and b encloses y, and also such that the distance between x and y lies between the limits $(2 \pm e)$ feet. It is evident, since e can be chosen as small as we please, that this statement exactly expresses the condition that A and B are two feet apart.

Straight Lines and Planes.—But the problem of the intellectual construction of straight lines and planes is not yet sufficiently analysed. We have interpreted the meaning of the statement that three or more points are collinear, and can similarly see how to interpret the meaning of the statement that four or more points are coplanar, in either case deriving the exact geometrical statements from vaguer statements respecting extended objects.

This procedure only contemplates groups of finite numbers of points. But straight lines and planes are conceived as containing infinite numbers of points. This completion of lines and planes is obtained by a renewed application of the principle of aggregation, just as a set of first crude thought-objects of perception are aggregated into one complete thought-object of perception. In this way repeated judgments of the collinearity of sets of points are finally, when certain conditions of interlacing are fulfilled, aggregated in the single judgment of all the points of the groups as forming one whole collinear group. Similarly for judgments of coplanarity. This process of logical aggregation can be exhibited in its exact logical analysis. But it is unnecessary here to proceed to such details. Thus we conceive our points as sorted into planes and straight lines, concerning which the various axioms of geometry hold. These axioms, in so far as they essentially require the conception of points, are capable of being exhibited as the outcome of vaguer, less exact judgments respecting the relations of extended objects.

Empty Space.—It must be observed that the points, hitherto defined, necessarily involve thought-objects of perception, and lie within the space-extension occupied by such objects. It is true that such objects are largely hypothetical, and that we can bring into our hypotheses sufficient objects to complete our lines and planes. But every such hypothesis weakens the connection between our scientific concept of nature and the actual observed facts which are involved in the actual sense-presentations.

Occam's razor, *Entia non multiplicanda præter necessitatem,* is not an arbitrary rule based on mere logical elegancy. Nor is its application purely confined to metaphysical speculation. I am ignorant of the precise reason for its metaphysical validity, but its scientific validity is obvious, namely, every use of hypothetical entities diminishes the claim of scientific reasoning to be the necessary outcome of a harmony between thought and sense-presentation. As hypothesis increases, necessity diminishes.

Commonsense thought also supports this refusal to conceive of all space as essentially depending on hypothetical objects which fill it. We think of material objects as filling space, but we ask whether any objects exist between the Earth and the Sun, between the stars, or beyond the stars. For us, space is there; the only question is whether or not it be full. But this form of question presupposes the meaning of empty space, namely, of space not containing hypothetical objects.

This brings up a wider use of the concept of points, necessitating a wider definition. Hitherto we have conceived points as indicating relations of enclosure between objects. We thus arrive at what now we will term " material points." But the idea of points can now be transformed so as to indicate the possibilities of external relations not those of enclosure. This is effected by an enlargement of the concept of ideal points, already known to geometers.

Define " material lines " to be complete collinear classes of collinear points. Consider now
the set of material lines which contain a certain
material point. Call such a set of lines an ideal
point. This set of lines indicates a possibility
of position, which is in fact occupied by that
material point common to all the material lines.
So this ideal point is an occupied ideal point.
Now consider a set of three material lines, such
that any two are coplanar, but not the whole
three, and further consider the complete set of
material lines such that each is coplanar with
each of the three material lines first chosen.
The axioms which hold for the material lines
will enable us to prove that any two lines of
this set are coplanar. Then the whole set of
lines, including the three original lines, forms an
ideal point, according to the definition in its full
generality. Such an ideal point may be occupied.
In that case there is a material point common
to all the lines of the set, but it may be un-
occupied. Then the ideal point merely indicates a possibility of spatial relations which has
not been realised. It is the point of empty
space. Thus the ideal points, which may or
may not be occupied, are the points of geometry
viewed as an applied science. These points are
distributed into straight lines and planes. But
any further discussion of this question will lead
us into the technical subject of the axioms of

N

geometry and their immediate consequences. Enough has been said to show how geometry arises according to the relational theory of space.

Space as thus conceived is the thought-space of the material world.

IV. Fields of Force

The thought-objects of science are conceived as directly related to this thought-space. Their spatial relations are among those indicated by the points of the thought-space. Their emergence in science has been merely a further development of processes already inherent in commonsense thought.

Relations within the complete sense-presentation were represented in thought by the concept of thought-objects of perception. All sense-presentation could not be represented in this way; also the change and disappearance of thought-objects occasioned confusion of thought. A reduction to order of this confusion was attempted by the concepts of permanent matter with primary and secondary qualities. Finally, this has issued in the secondary qualities being traced as perception of events generated by the objects, but—as perceived—entirely disconnected with them. Also the thought-objects of perception have been replaced by molecules and electrons and ether-waves, until at length it is never the thought-object of science which is perceived, but complicated series of events in which they are implicated. If science be right, nobody ever perceived a thing, but only an event. The result is, that the older language of philosophy which still survives in many quarters is now thoroughly confusing when brought into connection with the modern concepts of science. Philosophy—that is, the older philosophy—conceives the thing as directly perceived. According to scientific thought, the ultimate thing is never perceived, perception essentially issuing from a series of events. It is impossible to reconcile the two points of view.

The advantage of the modern scientific concept is that it is enabled to " explain " the fluid vague outlines of sense-presentation. The thought-object of perception is now conceived as a fairly stable state of motion of a huge group of molecules, constantly changing, but preserving a certain identity of characteristics. Also stray sense-objects, not immediately given as part of a thought-object of perception, are now explicable : the dancing light-reflection, the vaguely heard sound, the smell. In fact, the perceived events of the scientific world have the same general definition and lack of definition, and the same general stability and lack of stability, as the sense-objects of the complete sense-presentation or as the thought-objects of perception.

The thought-objects of science, namely, molecules, atoms, and electrons, have gained in permanence. The events are reduced to changes in space-configuration. The laws determining these changes are the ultimate laws of nature.

The laws of change in the physical universe proceed on the assumption that the preceding states of the universe determine the character of the change. Thus, to know the configurations and events of the universe up to and including any instant would involve sufficient data from which to determine the succession of events throughout all time.

But in tracing the antecedents of events, commonsense thought, dealing with the world of thought-objects of perception, habitually assumes that the greater number of antecedent events can be neglected as irrelevant. Consideration of causes is restricted to a few events during a short preceding interval. Finally, in scientific thought it has been assumed that the events in an arbitrarily small preceding duration are sufficient. Thus physical quantities and their successive differential co-efficients up to any order at the instant, but with their limiting values just before that instant, are on this theory sufficient to determine the state of the universe at all times after the instant. More particular laws are assumed. But the search for them is guided by this general principle. Also it is assumed that the greater number of events in the physical universe are irrelevant to the production of any particular effect, which is assumed to issue from relatively few antecedents. These assumptions have grown out of the experience of mankind. The first lesson of life is to concentrate attention on few factors of sense-presentations, and on still fewer of the universe of thought-objects of perception.

The principle by which—consciously or unconsciously—thought has been guided is that in searching for particular causes, remoteness in time and remoteness in space are evidences of comparative disconnection of influence. The extreme form of this principle is the denial of any action at a distance either in time or space. The difficulty in accepting this principle in its crude form is, that since there are no contiguous points, only coincident bodies can act on each other. I can see no answer to this difficulty—namely, either bodies have the same location and are thus coincident, or they have different locations and are thus at a distance and do not act on each other.

This difficulty is not evaded by the hypothesis of an ether, continuously distributed. For two reasons : in the first place, the continuity of the ether does not avoid the dilemma; and secondly, the difficulty applies to time as well as to space, and the dilemma would prove that causation producing change is impossible, namely, no changed condition could be the result of antecedent circumstances.

On the other hand, a direct interaction between two bodies separated in space undoubtedly offends the conception of distance as implying physical disconnection as well as spatial relation. There is no logical difficulty in the assumption of action at a distance as in the case of its denial, but it is contradictory to persistent assumptions of that apparatus of commonsense thought which it is the main business of science to harmonise with sense-presentation, employing only the minimum of modification.

Modern science is really unconcerned with this debate. Its (unacknowledged) conceptions are really quite different, though the verbal explanations retain the form of a previous epoch. The point of the change in conception is that the old thought-object of science was conceived as possessing a simplicity not belonging to the material universe as a whole. It was secluded within a finite region of space, and changes in its circumstances could only arise from forces which formed no essential part of its nature. An ether was called into existence to explain the active relations between these passive thought-objects. The whole conception suffers from the logical

difficulties noted above. Also no clear conception can be formed of the sense in which the
ether is explanatory. It is to possess a type of
activity denied to the original thought-object,
namely, it carries potential energy, whereas the
atom possessed only kinetic energy, the so-called
potential energy of an atom belonging really to
the surrounding ether. The truth is, that ether
is really excepted from the axiom " no action at
a distance," and the axiom thereby is robbed of
all its force.

The modern thought-object of science—not yet
explicitly acknowledged—has the complexity of
the whole material universe. In physics, as
elsewhere, the hopeless endeavour to derive
complexity from simplicity has been tacitly
abandoned. What is aimed at is not simplicity,
but persistence and regularity. In a sense regularity is a sort of simplicity. But it is the simplicity of stable mutual relations, and not the
simplicity of absence of types of internal structure
or of type of relation. This thought-object fills
all space. It is a " field "; that is to say, it is a
certain distribution of scalar and vector quantities
throughout space, these quantities having each
its value for each point of space at each point
of time, being continuously distributed throughout space and throughout time, possibly with
some exceptional discontinuities. The various
types of quantity which form the field have fixed

relations to each other at each point of time and space. These relations are the ultimate laws of nature.

For example, consider an electron. There is a scalar distribution of electricity, which is what is ordinarily called the electron. This scalar distribution has a volume-density ρ at the time t at any point (x, y, z). Thus ρ is a function of (x, y, z, t), which is zero except within a restricted region. Furthermore, at any time t, as an essential adjunct, there is a continuous space distribution at each point of the two vectors (X, Y, Z), which is the electric force, and (α, β, γ), which is the magnetic force. Lastly, individuality is ascribed to the scalar electric distribution, so that in addition to its conservation of quantity—involved in the assumed laws—it is also possible to assign the velocities with which the various individual parts of the distribution are moving. Let (u, v, w) be this velocity at (x, y, z, t).

This whole scheme of scalar and vector quantities, namely, ρ, (X, Y, Z), (α, β, γ), (u, v, w) is interconnected by the electromagnetic laws. It follows from these laws that the electron, in the sense of the scalar distribution ρ, is to be conceived as at each instant propagating from itself an emanation which travels outwards with the velocity of light *in vacuo*, and from which (X, Y, Z) and (α, β, γ) can be calculated, so far as they are due to that electron. Thus the field, at any time, due to the electron as a whole depends on the previous history of the electron, the nearer to the electron the more recent being the relevant history. The whole scheme of such a field is one single thought-object of science : the electron and its emanations form one essential whole, namely one thought-object of science, essentially complex and essentially filling all space. The electron proper, namely, the scalar distribution ρ, is the focus of the whole, the essential focal property being that the field at any instant is completely determined by the previous history of the focus and of its space relations through all previous time. But the field and the focus are not independent concepts, they are essentially correlated in one organised unity, namely, they are essentially correlated terms in the field of one relation in virtue of which the entities enter into our thoughts.

The fields of a group of electrons are superposed according to the linear law for aggregation, namely, pure addition for analogous scalar quantities and the parallelogram law for analogous vectors. The changes in motion of each electron depend entirely on the resultant field in the region it occupies. Thus a field can be viewed as a possibility of action, but a possibility which represents an actuality.

It is to be noted that the two alternative views of causation are here both included. The complete field within any region of space depends on the past histories of all the electrons, histories extending backwards in proportion to their distances. Also this dependence can be conceived as a transmission. But viewing the cause which effects changes on the electron within that region, it is solely that field within the region, which field is coincident with that electron both in time and in space.

This process of conceiving the actuality underlying a possibility is the uniform process by which regularity and permanence is introduced into scientific thought, namely, we proceed from the actuality of the fact to the actuality of possibility.

In conformity with this principle, propositions are the outgrowth from actual thought-expressions, thought-objects of perceptions from crude sense-objects, hypothetical thought-objects of perception from actual thought-objects of perception, material points from hypothetical infinite suites of hypothetical thought-objects of perception, ideal points from material points, thought-objects of science from thought-objects of perception, fields of electrons from actual mutual reactions of actual electrons.

The process is a research for permanence, uniformity, and simplicity of logical relation. But it does not issue in simplicity of internal structure. Each ultimate thought-object of science

retains every quality attributed to the whole
scientific universe, but retains them in a form
characterised by permanence and uniformity.

V. Conclusion

We commenced by excluding judgments of
worth and ontological judgments. We conclude
by recalling them. Judgments of worth are no
part of the texture of physical science, but they
are part of the motive of its production. Mankind have raised the edifice of science, because
they have judged it worth while. In other
words, the motives involve innumerable judgments of value. Again, there has been conscious
selection of the parts of the scientific field to be
cultivated, and this conscious selection involves
judgments of value. These values may be
æsthetic, or moral, or utilitarian, namely, judgments as to the beauty of the structure, or as
to the duty of exploring the truth, or as to
utility in the satisfaction of physical wants.
But whatever the motive, without judgments of
value there would have been no science.

Again, ontological judgments were not excluded
by reason of any lack of interest. They are in
fact presupposed in every act of life : in our
affections, in our self-restraints, and in our constructive efforts. They are presupposed in moral
judgments. The difficulty about them is the

absence of agreement as to the method of harmonising the crude judgments of common-sense.

Science does not diminish the need of a metaphysic. Where this need is most insistent is in connection with what above has been termed " the actuality underlying a possibility." A few words of explanation may render the argument clearer, although they involve a rash approach to metaphysical heights which it is not the purpose of this paper to explore.

The conception of subject and object in careless discussion covers two distinct relations. There is the relation of the whole perceiving consciousness to part of its own content, for example, the relation of a perceiving consciousness to an object of redness apparent to it. There is also the relation of a perceiving consciousness to an entity which does not exist in virtue of being part of the content of that consciousness. Such a relation, so far as known to the perceiving consciousness, must be an inferred relation, the inference being derived from an analysis of the content of the perceiving consciousness.

The bases for such inferences must be elements in consciousness directly known as transcending their immediate presentation in consciousness. Such elements are universal logical truths, moral and æsthetic truths, and truths embodied in hypothetical propositions. These are the immediate objects of perception which are other than the mere affections of the perceiving subject. They have the property of being parts of the immediate presentations for individual subjects and yet more than such parts. All other existence is inferred existence.

In this chapter we are more directly concerned with truths embodied in hypothetical propositions. Such truths must not be confused with any doubtfulness which attaches to our judgments of the future course of natural phenomena. A hypothetical proposition, like a categorical judgment, may or may not be doubtful. Also like a categorial judgment, it expresses a fact. This fact is twofold : as a presentation in consciousness, it is just this hypothetical judgment; as expressing a categorical fact, it states a relation which lies beyond consciousness, holding between entities thereby inferred.

But this metaphysical analysis, short though it be, is probably wrong, and at the best will only command very partial assent. Certainly; and this admission brings out the very point which I wished to make. Physical science is based on elements of thought, such as judgments registering actual perceptions, and judgments registering hypothetical perceptions which under certain circumstances would be realised.

These elements form the agreed content of the apparatus of commonsense thought. They require metaphysical analysis; but they are among the data from which metaphysics starts. A metaphysic which rejects them has failed, in the same way as physical science has failed when it is unable to harmonise them into its theory.

Science only renders the metaphysical need more urgent. In itself it contributes little directly to the solution of the metaphysical problem. But it does contribute something, namely, the exposition of the fact that our experience of sensible apparent things is capable of being analysed into a scientific theory, a theory not indeed complete, but giving every promise of indefinite expansion. This achievement emphasises the intimate relation between our logical thought and the facts of sensible apprehension. Also the special form of scientific theory is bound to have some influence. In the past false science has been the parent of bad metaphysics. After all, science embodies a rigorous scrutiny of one part of the whole evidence from which metaphysicians deduce their conclusions.

CHAPTER VIII

SPACE, TIME, AND RELATIVITY

(Paper read to Section A at the Manchester Meeting of the British Association, 1915, and later before the Aristotelian Society)

FUNDAMENTAL Problems concerning space and time have been considered from the standpoints created by many different sciences. The object of this paper is the humble one of bringing some of these standpoints into relation with each other. This necessitates a very cursory treatment of each point of view.

Mathematical physicists have evolved their theory of relativity to explain the negative results of the Morley-Michelson experiment and of the Trouton experiment. Experimental psychologists have considered the evolution of spatial ideas from the crude sense-data of experience. Metaphysicians have considered the majestic uniformity of space and time, without beginning and without end, without boundaries, and without exception in the truths concerning them; all these qualities the more arresting to our attention from the confused accidental nature

191

of the empirical universe which is conditioned by them. Mathematicians have studied the axioms of geometry, and can now deduce all that is believed to be universally true of space and of time by the strictest logic from a limited number of assumptions.

These various lines of thought have been evolved with surprisingly little interconnection. Perhaps it is as well. The results of science are never quite true. By a healthy independence of thought perhaps we sometimes avoid adding other people's errors to our own. But there can be no doubt that the normal method of cross-fertilising thought is by considering the same, or allied problems to our own, in the form which they assume in other sciences.

Here I do not propose to enter into a systematic study of these various chapters of science. I have neither the knowledge nor the time.

First, let us take the ultimate basis of any theory of relativity. All space measurement is from stuff in space to stuff in space. The geometrical entities of empty space never appear. The only geometrical properties of which we have any direct knowledge are properties of those shifting, changeable appearances which we call things in space. It is the sun which is distant, and the ball which is round, and the lamp-posts which are in linear order. Wherever mankind may have got its idea of an infinite unchangeable space from, it is safe to say that it is not an immediate deliverance of direct observation.

There are two antagonistic philosophical ways of recognising this conclusion.

One is to affirm that space and time are conditions for sensible experience, that without projection into space and time sensible experience would not exist. Thus, although it may be true to say that our knowledge of space and time is given in experience, it is not true to say that it is deduced from experience in the same sense that the Law of Gravitation is so deduced. It is not deduced, because in the act of experiencing we are necessarily made aware of space as an infinite given whole, and of time as an unending uniform succession. This philosophical position is expressed by saying that space and time are *a priori* forms of sensibility.

The opposed philosophical method of dealing with the question is to affirm that our concepts of time and space are deductions from experience, in exactly the same way as the Law of Gravitation is such a deduction. If we form exact concepts of points, lines and surfaces, and of successive instants of time, and assume them to be related as expressed by the axioms of geometry and the axioms for time, then we find that we have framed a concept which, with all the exactness of which our observations are capable, expresses the facts of experience.

o

These two philosophic positions are each designed to explain a certain difficulty. The *a priori* theory explains the absolute universality ascribed to the laws of space and time, a universality not ascribed to any deduction from experience. The experiential theory explains the derivation of the space-time concepts without introducing any other factors beyond those which are admittedly present in framing the other concepts of physical science.

But we have not yet done with the distinctions which in any discussion of space or time must essentially be kept in mind. Put aside the above question as to how these space-time concepts are related to experience—What are they when they are formed?

We may conceive of the points of space as self-subsistent entities which have the indefinable relation of being occupied by the ultimate stuff (matter, I will call it) which is there. Thus, to say that the sun is *there* (wherever it is) is to affirm the relation of occupation between the set of positive and negative electrons which we call the sun and a certain set of points, the points having an existence essentially independent of the sun. This is the absolute theory of space. The absolute theory is not popular just now, but it has very respectable authority on its side —Newton, for one—so treat it tenderly. The other theory is associated with Leibniz.

Our space concepts are concepts of relations between things in space. Thus there is no such entity as a self-subsistent point. A point is merely the name for some peculiarity of the relations between the matter which is, in common language, said to be in space.

It follows from the relative theory that a point should be definable in terms of the relations between material things. So far as I am aware, this outcome of the theory has escaped the notice of mathematicians, who have invariably assumed the point as the ultimate starting ground of their reasoning. Many years ago I explained some types of ways in which we might achieve such a definition, and more recently have added some others. Similar explanations apply to time. Before the theories of space and time have been carried to a satisfactory conclusion on the relational basis, a long and careful scrutiny of the definitions of points of space and instants of time will have to be undertaken, and many ways of effecting these definitions will have to be tried and compared. This is an unwritten chapter of mathematics, in much the same state as was the theory of parallels in the eighteenth century.

In this connection I should like to draw attention to the analogy between time and space. In analysing our experience we distinguish events, and we also distinguish things whose changing relations form the events. If I had time it would be interesting to consider more closely these concepts of events and of things. It must suffice now to point out that things have certain relations to each other which we consider as relations between the space extensions of the things; for example, one space can contain the other, or exclude it, or overlap it. A point in space is nothing else than a certain set of relations between spatial extensions.

Analogously, there are certain relations between events which we express by saying that they are relations between the temporal durations of these events, that is, between the temporal extensions of the events. [The durations of two events A and B may one precede the other, or may partially overlap, or may one contain the other, giving in all six possibilities.] The properties of the extension of an event in time are largely analogous to the extension of an object in space. Spatial extensions are expressed by relations between objects, temporal extensions by relations between events.

The point in time is a set of relations between temporal extensions. It needs very little reflection to convince us that a point in time is no direct deliverance of experience. We live in durations, and not in points. But what community, beyond the mere name, is there between extension in time and extension in space? In view of the intimate connection between time and space revealed by the modern theory of relativity, this question has taken on a new importance.

I have not thought out an answer to this question. I suggest, however, that time and space embody those relations between objects on which depends our judgment of their externality to ourselves. Namely, location in space and location in time both embody and perhaps necessitate a judgment of externality. This suggestion is very vague, and I must leave it in this crude form.

Diverse Euclidean Measure Systems

Turning now to the mathematical investigations on the axioms of geometry, the outcome, which is most important for us to remember, is the great separation which it discloses between non-metrical projective geometry, and metrical geometry. Non-metrical projective geometry is by far the more fundamental. Starting with the concepts of points, straight lines, and planes (of which not all three need be taken as indefinable), and with certain very simple non-metrical properties of these entities—such as, for instance, that two points uniquely determine a straight line—nearly the whole of geometry can be constructed. Even quantitative co-ordinates can be introduced, to facilitate the reasoning. But no mention of distance, area, or volume, need have been introduced.   Points will have an order on the line, but order does not imply any settled distance.

When we now inquire what measurements of distance are possible, we find that there are different systems of measurement all equally possible.   There are three main types of system : any system of one type gives Euclidean geometry, any system of another type gives Hyperbolic (or Lobatchewskian) geometry, any system of the third type gives Elliptic geometry. Also different beings, or the same being if he chooses, may reckon in different systems of the same type, or in systems of different types.   Consider the example which will interest us later.   Two beings, A and B, agree to use the same three intersecting lines as axes of x, y, z.   They both employ a system of measurement of the Euclidean type, and (what is not necessarily the case) agree as to the plane at infinity.   That is, they agree as to the lines which are parallel.   Then with the usual method of rectangular Cartesian axes, they agree that the coordinates of P are the lengths ON, NM, MP. So far all is harmony. A fixes on the segment OU_1, on Ox, as being the unit length, and B on the segment OV_1, on Ox.   A calls his coordinates (x,y,z), and B calls them (X,Y,Z).

Then it is found [since both systems are Euclidean] that, whatever point P be taken,

$$X = \beta x, \; Y = \gamma y, \; Z = \delta z. \quad [\beta \neq \gamma \neq \delta.]$$

They proceed to adjust their differences, and first take the x-coordinates. Obviously they have taken different units of length along Ox. The length OU_1, which A calls one unit, B calls β units. B changes his unit length to OU_1, from its original length OV_1, and obtains $X = x$. But now, as he must use the same unit for all his measurements, his other coordinates are altered in the same ratio. Thus we now have

$$X = x, \; Y = \gamma y/\beta, \; Z = \delta z/\beta.$$

The fundamental divergence is now evident. A and B agree as to their units along Ox. They settled that by taking along that axis a given segment OU_1 as having the unit length. But they cannot agree as to what segment along Oy is equal to OU_1. A says it is OU_2, and B that it is OU_2'. Similarly for lengths along OZ.

The result is that A's spheres

$$x^2 + y^2 + z^2 = r^2,$$

are B's ellipsoids,

$$X^2 + \beta^2 Y^2/\gamma^2 + \beta^2 Z^2/\delta^2 = r^2,$$

i. e. $\qquad X^2/\beta^2 + Y^2/\gamma^2 + Z^2/\delta^2 = r^2/\beta^2.$

Thus the measurement of angles by the two is hopelessly at variance.

If $\beta \neq \gamma \neq \delta$, there is one, and only one, set of common rectangular axes at O, namely that from which they started. If $\gamma = \delta$, but $\beta \neq \gamma$, then there are a singly infinite number of common rectangular axes found by rotating the axes round Ox. This is, for us, the interesting case. The same phenomena are reproduced by transferring to any parallel axes.

The root of the difficulty is, that A's measuring rod, which for him is a rigid invariable body, appears to B as changing in length when turned in different directions. Similarly all measuring rods, satisfactory to A, violate B's immediate judgment of invariability, and change according to the same law. There is no way out of the difficulty. Two rods ρ and σ coincide whenever laid one on the other; ρ is held still, and both men agree that it does not change. But σ is turned round. A says it is invariable, B says it changes To test the matter, ρ is turned round to measure it, and exactly fits it. But while A is satisfied, B declares that ρ has changed in exactly the same way as did σ. Meanwhile B has procured two material rods satisfactory to him as invariable, and A makes exactly the same objections.

We shall say that A and B employ diverse Euclidean metrical systems.

The most extraordinary fact of human life is that all beings seem to form their judgments of spatial quantity according to the same metrical system.

Relativity in Modern Physics

Owing to the fact that points of space are incapable of direct recognition, there is a difficulty—apart from any abstract question of the nature of space—in deciding on the motion to be ascribed to any body. Even if there be such a thing as absolute position, it is impossible in practice to decide directly whether a body's absolute position has changed. All spatial measurement is relative to matter.

Newton's laws of motion in their modern dress evade this difficulty by asserting that a framework of axes of coordinates can be defined by their relations to matter such that, assuming these axes to be at rest, and all velocities to be measured relatively to them, the laws hold. The same expedient has to be employed for time, namely, the laws hold when the measurement of the flow of time is made by the proper reference to periodic events. Thus the laws assert that the framework and the natural clock adapted for their use have been successfully found.

But, if one framework will do, an infinity of others serve equally well; namely, not only—as is of course the case—all those at rest relatively to the first framework, but also all those which move without relative rotation with uniform velocity relatively to the first. This whole set of frameworks is on a level in respect to Newton's laws. We will call them Dynamical frameworks.

Now, suppose there are two observers, A and B. They agree in their non-metrical projective geometry, *e.g.*, what A calls a straight line so does B. They also both apply a Euclidean metrical system of measurement to this space. Their two metrical systems also agree in having the same plane at infinity, that is, lines which are parallel for A are also parallel for B. Furthermore, they have both successfully applied Newton's laws to the movement of matter, and agree in having the same sets of dynamical axes. But the framework (among these sets) which A chooses to regard as at rest is different from the frame (among the same sets) which B so regards.

Without alteration of their respective judgment of rest, they choose their coordinate axes so that the origins (O for A, and O' for B) are in relative motion along OO', which is the axis of *x* for both.

Further, since OO' is the line of symmetry of their diverse Euclidean systems, we assume that the two measure-systems agree for planes perpendicular to OO', *i.e.*, we assume a symmetry round OO'. Then if, for A at O, the distance OO' be ξ, the relations at any instant between A's coordinates (x, y, z) and B's coordinates

(x',y',x') for the same point P are given by

$$x' = \beta(x - \xi), \ y' = y, \ z' = z.$$

Also, according to A's clock, O' is moving forward with a uniform velocity v, and we measure A's time from the instant of the coincidence of O and O'.

Thus $$\xi = vt,$$
and

$$x' = \beta(x - vt), \ y' = y, \ z' = z.$$

We now consider B's clock, and ask for the most general supposition which is consistent with the fact that their judgments as to the fact of uniform motion are in agreement.

We do not assume that events in various parts of space which A considers to be simultaneous are so considered by B. But we assume that at any point P, with coordinates (x,y,z) for A, there is a determinate relation between B's time T and x, y, z, t.

Put $$T = f(x,y,z,t).$$
Write

$$P = \frac{\delta T}{\delta x}, \ Q = \frac{\delta T}{\delta y}, \ R = \frac{\delta T}{\delta z}, \ S = \frac{\delta T}{\delta t}.$$

Now suppose that the point P is moving, and that (u_1, u_2, u_3) is its set of component velocities along the axes according to A's " space and clock " system, and (U_1, U_2, U_3) is its set of component velocities according to B's " space and clock" system. Then by mere differentiation it follows after a short mathematical deduction that

$$U_1 = \left\{\frac{d\beta}{dt}(x - vt) + \beta(u_1 - v)\right\} \Big/ \{Pu_1 + Qu_2 + Ru_3 + S\},$$

$$U_2 = u_2 / \{Pu_1 + Qu_2 + Ru_3 + S\},$$

$$U_3 = u_3 / \{Pu_1 + Qu_2 + Ru_3 + S\}.$$

But we have assumed that, whatever the direction of the resultant velocity (u_1, u_2, u_3), the velocities (U_1, U_2, U_3) and (u_1, u_2, u_3) are both uniform when either is uniform.

Hence it is easily proved that β, P, Q, R, S are independent of the coordinates (x, y, z) and of the time t. In other words, they are constant.

Hence we obtain

$$U_1 = \beta(u_1 - v) / \{Pu_1 + Qu_2 + Ru_3 + S\},$$

and $\quad\quad T = Px + Qy + Rz + St.$

But we assumed that OO′, i.e., Ox, is an axis of symmetry. It follows from this assumption that

$$Q = R = 0.$$

We thus obtain the simplified results

$$\left.\begin{array}{l} T = Px + St, \\ U_1 = \beta(u_1 - v)/(Pu_1 + S), \\ U_2 = u_2/(Pu_1 + S), \\ U_3 = u_3/(Pu_1 + S). \end{array}\right\} \quad \text{(I)}$$

Here we remember that (u_1, u_2, u_3) are the velocities of any particle according to A's " space and clock " system, and that (U_1, U_2, U_3) are the velocities of the same point according to B's

" space and clock " system. We have obtained
the most general relations consistent with the
facts that (1) they both employ Euclidean
systems, related as described above, and (2) they
agree in their judgments on the uniformity of
velocity.

We now compare their judgments on the magni-
tudes of velocities.

Let the magnitude of the velocity of P be V
according to A's judgment, and V′ according to
B's′ judgment.

Then

$$V^2 = u_1{}^2 + u_2{}^2 + u_3{}^2,$$
$$V'^2 = U_1{}^2 + U_2{}^2 + U_3{}^2.$$

Also we can put

$$u_1 = lV, \quad u_2 = mV, \quad u_3 = nV,$$

where (l, m, n) have nothing to do with the magnitude V, but simply depend on the direction of
motion. In fact (l, m, n), are the " direction
cosines " of the velocity according to A's judgment. By substituting in the above equation
for V^2 we see that

$$l^2 + m^2 + n^2 = 1.$$

Now, substituting for (u_1, u_2, u_3) in the equations (I) above, and squaring and adding, and
eliminating $m^2 + n^2$ by the relation just found,
we at once find

$$V'^2 = \frac{(\beta^2 - 1)V^2 l^2 - 2\beta^2 Vvl + \beta^2 v^2 + V^2}{(PVl + S)^2}.$$

It is thus seen that in general the relation of V' to V depends on the direction cosine l. Now l is the cosine of the angle which the direction of the velocity V makes with Ox, according to A's judgment.

The meaning of this relation is, that if A discharges, from guns at the point P, shells with a given muzzle velocity V according to his judgment, B will consider that their muzzle velocities are different from each other, except in the case of pairs of guns equally inclined to the axis OO'. Instances of this type of diversity of judgment can be noted any day by any one who looks out of the window of a railway carriage, and forgets that he is travelling.

Now, suppose the velocity V' bears a relation to the velocity V, which is independent of l. Then l must disappear from the above formula. There are two conditions to be satisfied

One condition is

$$V^2 = \beta^2 v^2 / (\beta^2 - 1),$$

or in a more convenient form

$$\beta^2 = 1/(1 - v^2/V^2).$$

The meaning of this condition is, that there is one, and only one, muzzle velocity V (according to A's judgment), namely, the muzzle velocity given by the above formula, which can have the property that B will judge that all the guns are firing in their diverse directions with one common muzzle velocity.

Let us now suppose that V has this peculiar value : that is, if we look on this value V as known, we must suppose that β is given by the second of the above formulæ.

The other condition allows P and S to be put in the forms

$$P = - \beta v / \lambda V^2, \quad S = \beta / \lambda,$$

where
$$V' = \lambda V.$$

Thus we have the bundle of formulæ

$$\beta^2 = 1/(1 - v^2/V^2),$$
$$T = \beta\{t - vx/V^2\}/\lambda,$$
$$V' = \lambda V.$$

The value which we give to λ is purely a matter for the adjustment of units. If we want A and B to agree in their judgments of the magnitude of this peculiar muzzle-velocity, we put $\lambda = 1$.

We then get the formulæ usually adopted, namely

$$\left.\begin{array}{l} \beta^2 = 1/(1 - v^2/V^2), \\ T = \beta\{t - vx/V^2\}, \\ V' = V. \end{array}\right\} \qquad \text{(II)}$$

But if we prefer that A and B should reckon (according to A's judgment) in the same units of time, we put $\lambda = \beta$, and obtain

$$\beta^2 = 1/(1 - v^2/V^2),$$
$$T = t - vx/V^2,$$
$$V' = \beta V.$$

But A and B are in any case in such hopeless difficulties over their comparisons of time-judgments that the detail of using the same units does not help them much. Accordingly the formulæ marked (II) are those used. Thus A and B agree in their judgments as to the magnitude of one special velocity V, whatever may be the direction in which the entity possessing it is moving.

In order to reach this measure of agreement, they have to disagree as to their space judgments and their time judgments. The root cause of their disagreement is their diverse judgment as to which axis system is to be taken at rest for the purpose of measuring velocities.

Before discussing the nature of the disagreement disclosed in formula (II), let us ask why we should bring these difficulties on our heads by supposing that two people in relative motion, who both (for the purpose of measuring velocities) assume that they are at rest, should agree in their judgments in respect to this special velocity V.

Such an agreement has no counterpart in any of our obvious judgments made from railway carriages. Surely we can wait till the contingency occurs before discussing the confusion which it creates.

But the contingency has occurred. It occurs

when we consider the velocity of light.   Perhaps I may venture to remind a philosophical society that light moves so very quickly that it is difficult to consider its velocity at all.   So we need not be surprised that this peculiar fact concerning its velocity is not more obvious.

Now V being the velocity of light, unless v is large, v/V (and still more v^2/V^2) will be quite inappreciable. The only velocity ready to hand which is big enough to give v/V an appreciable value is the velocity of the earth in its orbit.

Many diverse experiments have been made, and they all agree in concluding that a man who assumes the earth to be at rest will find by measurement that the velocity of light is the same in all directions. Furthermore, when the same man turns his attention to interstellar or interplanetary phenomena, and assumes the sun to be at rest, he will again find the velocity of light to be the same in all directions. These are well-attested experiments made at long intervals of time.

This is the exact contingency contemplated above.

Again the velocity of light *in vacuo* has recently taken on a new dignity. It used to be one among other wave velocities such as the velocity of sound in air, or in water, or the velocity of surface waves in water. But Clerk Maxwell

P

discovered that all electromagnetic influences are propagated with the velocity of light, and now modern physical science half suspects that electromagnetic influences are the only physical influences which relate the changes in the physical world. Accordingly the velocity of light becomes the fundamental natural velocity, and experiment shows that our judgment of its magnitude is not affected by our choice of the framework at rest, so long as we keep to a set of dynamical axes. These experiments on light have been confirmed by other electromagnetic experiments not involving light.

Thus we are driven to equations (II), where **V** is the velocity of light.

The first conclusion to be drawn from equations (II) is that two people who make different choices of bodies at rest will disagree as to their measuring rods in the way described above. There is no peculiar difficulty about that. The only wonder is that all people agree so well in their judgments as to metrical systems. A mathematical angel would naturally expect incarnate men to be in violent disagreement on this subject.

But the case of time is different. For simplicity of statement we speak of A as at O, and B as at O'. We remember that O' is moving relatively to O with velocity v in direction OO'. Suppose A and B are looking in this direction; and they both measure their time from the instant when they met, as O' passed over O. Then we have

$$\mathbf{T} = \{t - vx/\mathbf{V}^2\}/\{1 - v^2/\mathbf{V}^2\}.$$

Now, suppose we consider all the events all over space which A considers to have happened simultaneously at the time t. The events of this set which occurred anywhere on a plane perpendicular to OO' at a distance x in front of O (according to A's reckoning), will have occurred according to B's reckoning at the time $\mathbf{T}$ as given above. Let us fix our attention on the fact that B does not consider all these events to be simultaneous. For let $\mathbf{T}_1$ and $\mathbf{T}_2$ be B's times for such events on planes x_1 and x_2. Then

$$\mathbf{T}_1 - \mathbf{T}_2 = v(x_2 - x_1)/(\mathbf{V}^2 - v^2).$$

Thus if x_2 be greater than x_1, $\mathbf{T}_2$ is less than $\mathbf{T}_1$. Thus B judges the more distant events in front of him to have happened earlier than the nearer events in front of him, and *vice versa* for the events behind. This disturbance of the judgment of simultaneity is the fundamental fact. Obviously the measurement of time intervals is a detail compared to simultaneity. A may think a sermon long, and B may think it short, but at least they should both agree that it stopped when the clock hand pointed at the hour. The worst of the matter is that so far as any test can be applied there is no method of discriminating between the validities of their judgments.

Thus we are confronted with two distinct concepts of the common world, A's space-time concept, and B's space-time concept. Who is right ? It is no use staying for an answer. We must follow the example of the wise old Roman, and pass on to other things.

Thus estimates of quantity in space and time, and, to some extent, even estimates of order, depend on the individual observer. But what are the crude deliverances of sensible experience, apart from that world of imaginative reconstruction which for each of us has the best claim to be called our real world ? Here the experimental psychologist steps in. We cannot get away from him. I wish we could, for he is frightfully difficult to understand. Also, sometimes his knowledge of the principles of mathematics is rather weak, and I sometimes suspect—— No, I will not say what I sometimes think : probably he, with equal reason, is thinking the same sort of thing of us.

I will, however, venture to summarise conclusions, which are, I believe, in harmony with the experimental evidence, both physical and psychological, and which are certainly suggested by the materials for that unwritten chapter in mathematical logic which I have already commended to your notice. The concepts of space and time and of quantity are capable of analysis into bundles of simpler concepts. In any given sensible experience it is not necessary, or even usual, that the whole complete bundle of such concepts apply. For example, the concept of externality may apply without that of linear order, and the concept of linear order may apply without that of linear distance.

Again, the abstract mathematical concept of a space-relation may confuse together distinct concepts which apply to the given perceptions. For example, linear order in the sense of a linear projection from the observer is distinct from linear order in the sense of a row of objects stretching across the line of sight.

Mathematical physics assumes a given world of definitely related objects, and the various space-time systems are alternative ways of expressing those relations as concepts in a form which also applies to the immediate experience of observers.

Yet there must be one way of expressing the relations between objects in a common external world. Alternative methods can only arise as the result of alternative standpoints; that is to say, as the result of leaving something added by the observer sticking (as it were) in the universe.

But this way of conceiving the world of physical science, as composed of hypothetical objects, leaves it as a mere fairy tale. What is really actual are the immediate experiences. The task of deductive science is to consider the concepts

which apply to these data of experience, and then
to consider the concepts relating to these concepts, and so on to any necessary degree of
refinement. As our concepts become more abstract, their logical relations become more general,
and less liable to exception. By this logical
construction we finally arrive at conceptions, (i)
which have determinate exemplifications in the
experience of the individuals, and (ii) whose
logical relations have a peculiar smoothness.
For example, conceptions of mathematical time,
of mathematical space, are such smooth conceptions. No one lives in " an infinite given
whole," but in a set of fragmentary experiences.
The problem is to exhibit the concepts of mathematical space and time as the necessary outcome
of these fragments by a process of logical building
up. Similarly for the other physical concepts.
This process builds a common world of conceptions out of fragmentary worlds of experience.
The material pyramids of Egypt are a conception, what is actual are the fragmentary experiences of the races who have gazed on them.

So far as science seeks to rid itself of hypothesis,
it cannot go beyond these general logical constructions. For science, as thus conceived, the
divergent time orders considered above present
no difficulty. The different time systems simply
register the different relations of the mathematical construct to those individual experiences

(actual or hypothetical) which could exist as the crude material from which the construct is elaborated.

But after all it should be possible so to elaborate the mathematical construct so as to eliminate specific reference to particular experiences. Whatever be the data of experience, there must be something which can be said of them as a whole, and that something is a statement of the general properties of the common world. It is hard to believe that with proper generalisation time and space will not be found among such properties.

Commentary added on reading the Paper before the Aristotelian Society

The first six pages of the paper consist of a summary of ideas which ought to be in our minds while considering problems of time and space. The ideas are mostly philosophical, and the summary has been made by an amateur in that science; so there is no reason to ascribe to it any importance except that of a modest reminder. There are only two points in this summary to which I would draw attention.

On pp. 192 and 193 there occurs—

" Wherever mankind . . . unending uniform succession."

If I understand Kant rightly—which I admit

to be very problematical—he holds that in the act of experience we are aware of space and time as ingredients necessary for the occurrence of experience. I would suggest—rather timidly—that this doctrine should be given a different twist, which in fact turns it in the opposite direction—namely, that in the act of experience we perceive a whole formed of related differentiated parts. The relations between these parts possess certain characteristics, and time and space are the expressions of some of the characteristics of these relations. Then the generality and uniformity which are ascribed to time and space express what may be termed the uniformity of the texture of experience.

The success of mankind—modest though it is—in deducing uniform laws of nature is, so far as it goes, a testimony that this uniformity of texture goes beyond those characteristics of the data of experience which are expressed as time and space. Time and space are necessary to experience in the sense that they are characteristics of our experience; and, of course, no one can have our experience without running into them. I cannot see that Kant's deduction amounts to much more than saying that " what is, is "—true enough, but not very helpful.

But I admit that what I have termed the " uniformity of the texture of experience " is a most curious and arresting fact. I am quite ready to believe that it is a mere illusion; and later on in the paper I suggest that this uniformity does not belong to the immediate relations of the crude data of experience, but is the result of substituting for them more refined logical entities, such as relations between relations, or classes of relations, or classes of classes of relations. By this means it can be demonstrated— I think—that the uniformity which must be ascribed to experience is of a much more abstract attenuated character than is usually allowed. This process of lifting the uniform time and space of the physical world into the status of logical abstractions has also the advantage of recognising another fact, namely, the extremely fragmentary nature of all direct individual experience.

My point in this respect is that fragmentary individual experiences are all that we know, and that all speculation must start from these *disjecta membra* as its sole datum. It is not true that we are directly aware of a smooth running world, which in our speculations we are to conceive as given. In my view the creation of the world is the first unconscious act of speculative thought; and the first task of a self-conscious philosophy is to explain how it has been done.

There are roughly two rival explanations. One is to assert the world as a postulate. The other way is to obtain it as a deduction, not a deduction through a chain of reasoning, but a deduction through a chain of definitions which, in fact, lifts thought on to a more abstract level in which the logical ideas are more complex, and their relations are more universal. In this way the broken limited experiences sustain that connected infinite world in which in our thoughts we live. There are three more remarks while on this point I wish to make—

(i) The fact that immediate experience is capable of this deductive superstructive must mean that it itself has a certain uniformity of texture. So this great fact still remains.

(ii) I do not wish to deny the world as a postulate. Speaking without prejudice, I do not see how in our present elementary state of philosophical advance we can get on without middle axioms, which, in fact, we habitually assume.

My position is, that by careful scrutiny we should extrude such postulates from every part of our organised knowledge in which it is possible to do without them.

Now, physical science organises our knowledge of the relations between the deliverances of our various senses. I hold that in this department of knowledge such postulates, though not entirely to be extruded, can be reduced to a minimum in the way which I have described.

I have not the slightest knowledge of theories respecting our emotions, affections, and moral sentiments, and I can well believe that in dealing with them further postulates are required. And in practice I recognise that we all make such postulates, uncritically.

(iii) The next paragraphs on pp. 193 and 194 are as follows—

" The opposed philosophical method . . . physical science."

It will be noted that, in the light of what has just been stated, the first of these paragraphs (which, I hope, faithfully expresses the experiential way of approaching the problem) really obscures the point which I have been endeavouring to make. The phrase, " If we form the exact concepts of points, etc.," is fatally ambiguous as between the method of postulating entities with assigned relations, and the method of forming logical constructions, and thus reaching points, etc., as the result of a chain of definitions.

Turning now to pp. 194–195, we come to the following paragraphs—

" The other theory . . . eighteenth century."

We note again that the relational theory of space from another point of view brings us back to the idea of the fundamental space-entities as being logical constructs from the relations between things. The difference is, that this paragraph is written from a more developed

point of view, as it implicitly assumes the things
in space, and conceives space as an expression
of certain of their relations. Combining this
paragraph with what has gone before, we see
that the suggested procedure is first to define
" things " in terms of the data of experience,
and then to define space in terms of the relations
between things.

This procedure is explicitly assumed in the
next short paragraph : " In this connection . . .
from the events."

The gist of the remaining paragraphs of this
section is contained in the paragraph at the
bottom of p. 196 : " The point in time . . . new
importance."

The sentence, " We live in durations, and not
in points," can be amplified by the addition,
" We live in space-extensions and not in space-
points."

It must be noted that " whole and part " as
applied to extensions in space or time must be
different from the " all and some " of logic, unless
we admit points to be the fundamental entities.
For " spatial whole and spatial part " can only
mean " all and some " if they really mean " all
the points and some of the points." But if
extensions and their relations are more fundamental than points, this interpretation is pre-
cluded. I suggest that " spatial whole and
spatial part " is intimately connected with the

fundamental relation between things from which
our space ideas spring.

The relation of space whole to space part has
many formal properties which are identical with
the properties of " all and some." Also when
points have been defined, we can replace it by
the conception of " all the points and some of the
points." But the confusion between the two
relations is fatal to sound views on the subject.

Diverse Euclidean Measure Systems

The next section deals with the measure
systems applicable to space.

A measure system is a group of congruent
transformations of space into itself. Consider a
rigid body occupying all space. Let this body
be moved in any way so that the particles of the
body which occupied points P_1, P_2, P_3, etc., now
occupy points Q_1, Q_2, Q_3, etc. Then any point
P_1 in space in uniquely related to the corresponding point Q_1 in space by a one-to-one transformation with certain characteristics. By the
aid of these transformations we can achieve the
definition of distance in a way which definitely
determines the distance between any two points,
provided that we can define what we mean by a
congruent transformation without introducing
the idea of distance. If we introduced the
idea of distance, we should simply say that a

congruent transformation is one which leaves all distances unchanged, *i. e.*, if P_1, P_2 are transformed into Q_1, Q_2 then the distance P_1P_2 is equal to the distance Q_1Q_2.

But mathematicians have succeeded in defining congruent transformations without any reference to distance.

There are alternative groups of such congruent transformations, and each group gives a different measure system for space. The distance P_1P_2 may equal the distance Q_1Q_2 for one measure system, and will not equal it for another measure system. All these different measure systems are on the same level, equally applicable. A being with a strong enough head could think of them all at once as applying to space. The result so far as it interests us in respect to the theory of relativity is explained on pp. 197–200, ending with "The most extraordinary fact . . . same metrical system." This final sentence bears on Poincaré's assertion that the measure system adopted is purely "conventional." I presume that by "conventional" a certain arbitrariness of choice is meant; and in that case, I must express entire dissent. It is true that within the circle of geometrical ideas there is no means of giving any preference to any one measure system, and any one is as good as any other. But it is not true that if we look at a normal carriage wheel, and at an oval curve one foot broad and ten feet long, we experience any arbitrariness of judgment in deciding which has approximately the form of a circle. Accordingly to Poincaré the choice between them, as representing a circle, is entirely conventional.

Again, we equally form immediate judgments as to whether a body is approximately rigid. We know that a paving stone is rigid, and that a concertina is not rigid. This again necessitates a determinate measure system, selected from among the others.

Accordingly we conclude that (i) each being does, in fact, employ a determinate measure system, which remains the same, except possibly for very small variations, and (ii) the measure systems of different human beings agree, to within the limits of our observations. These conclusions are not the less extraordinary because no plain man has ever doubted them.

It is an interesting subject to investigate exactly what are the fundamental uniformities of experience which necessitate this conclusion. It is not so easy as it looks, since we have to divest ourselves of all aid of scientific hypothesis if our conclusions are to be demonstrative.

Relativity in Modern Physics

Pp. 201–202, " Owing to the fact . . . which B so regards."

The fundamental formulæ for the theory of relativity are the relations between diverse co-ordinate systems given on p. 203, and formulæ II at the bottom of p. 207. The general explanation of one method in which these formulæ arise—namely, Einstein's method—is given on pp. 201–211. Namely, we seek the condition that for all dynamical axes the velocity of light should be the same, and the same in all directions. It should be noted that the experiments which, so far as they go, confirm these formulæ, can also be explained in another way which makes the theory of relativity unnecessary. We need only ascribe to the ether a certain property of contraction in the direction of motion, and the thing is done. So no one need be bludgeoned into accepting the rather bizarre doctrine of relativity, nor indeed any other scientific generalisation. The good old homely ether, which we all know, can in this case serve the purpose. Just as an author of genius, if he lives long enough, survives the inevitable accusation of immorality, so the ether by dint of persistence has outlived all reputation of extravagance. But if we detach ourselves from the glib phraseology concerning it, the scientific ether is uncommonly like the primitive explanation of the soul, as a little man inside us, which can sometimes be caught escaping in the form of a butterfly. As soon as the ether has to be patched up with special properties to explain special experiments, its scientific use is problematical, and its philosophic use is *nil*.

Philosophically the ether seems to me to be an ambitious attempt to give a complete explanation of the physical universe by making an elephant stand on a tortoise. Scientifically it has a perfectly adequate use by veiling the extremely abstract character of scientific generalisations under a myth, which enables our imaginations to work more freely. I am not advocating the extrusion of ether from our scientific phraseology, even though at special points we have to abandon it.

But the key to the reasons why it is worth while to consider seriously the doctrine of relativity is to be found on pp. 209, 210 : " Again the velocity of light . . . not involving light." Namely, we have begun to suspect that all physical influences require time for their propagation in space. This generalisation is a long way from being proved. Gravitation stands like a lion in the path. But if it be the case, then all idea of an immediate presentation to us of an aspect of the world as it in fact is, must necessarily be abandoned. What we perceive at any instant is already ancient history, with the dates of the various parts hopelessly mixed.

We must add to this the difficulty of determining what is at rest and what is in motion, and the further difficulty of determining a definite

Q

uniform flow of time. It is no use discussing this matter as though, but for the silly extravagant doctrine of relativity, everything would be plain sailing. It isn't. You may be quite sure that when, after prolonged study, you endeavour to give the simplest explanation of a grave difficulty, you will be accused of extravagance. I have no responsibility for the doctrine of relativity, and hold no brief for it, but it has some claim to be considered as a comparatively simple way out of a scientific maze.

In the first place, we use the Newtonian dynamical sets of axes, and the Newtonian clock to extricate ourselves partially from the difficulties of rest, motion, and time. These have proved capable of scientific determination within the limits of our experimental accuracy. Thus the only thing left over is the choice of the axes at rest, which is a completely indeterminate problem on Newtonian principles.

Again, so far as we can at present guess by adopting the theory that all metrical influence is electromagnetic, all influences are propagated with the velocity of light *in vacuo*. This electromagnetic hypothesis is by no means established, but it gives the simplest of all possible results in respect to the propagation of influence, which we therefore adopt.

But what dynamical axes are we taking as at rest? Now our practical choice gives a range of relative velocities small compared to that of light. So except for certain refined experiments it does not matter. There are two possibilities—

(i) We may assume that one set of axes are at rest, and that the others will show traces of motion in respect to the velocity of light; or—

(ii) That the velocity of light is the same in all directions whichever be the dynamical axes assumed.

The first supposition is negatived by experiment, and hence we are driven to the second supposition; which immediately lands us in the whole theory of relativity.

But if we will not have this theory we must reject the earlier supposition that the velocity of light *in vacuo* is the same in all directions. This we do, in fact, by assuming an ether, and assuming a certain law for its modification. Then we, in fact, adopt the first supposition so far as to hold that there are dynamical axes specially at rest, namely, at rest relatively to the undisturbed ether. Then an assumed law for the modification of the ether so alters the velocity of light that we explain why no dynamical axes show traces of motion.

I wish now to go back to the point which I made a few minutes ago, that what we perceive at any instant is ancient history with its dates hopelessly mixed. In the earlier part of my comments I emphasised the point that our only data as to the physical world are our sensible perceptions. We must not slip into the fallacy of assuming that we are comparing a given world with given perceptions of it. The physical world is in some general sense of the term a deduced concept.

Our problem is, in fact, to fit the world to our perceptions, and not our perceptions to the world.